JN065992

Phase 1
CONTENTS

Phase 2
VISUALS

Power Presentation
[New Edition]

Phase 3
DELIVERY

Phase 4
INTERACTION

JACET 関西支部教材開発研究会
JACET Material Design & Development SIG

SANSHUSHA

●はしがき

　本書は、ロングセラー『英語でプレゼンテーション』*Power Presentation* の改訂新版です。前作が構想された時点では、英語のプレゼンテーションについての教科書はほぼ皆無に等しく、プレゼンテーションはまだスピーチや上級スピーキングという特殊な授業で扱われていました。それから約 20 年後の今日、前作で紹介した PowerPoint の使用率も増加し、YouTube や Zoom など web 情報配信ツールも多様化しています。プレゼンテーションに関する大学生向け教科書や一般書も年々増え、プレゼンテーションは一般的な英語の授業でも取り入れられるようになってきました。

　本書は、前作の長所を活かしながらも、こうしたプレゼンテーションを巡る情勢変化を考慮し、基盤となるコンセプトから一新しました。それはプレゼンテーションを舞台芸術に見立て、Phase（段階・局面）を追って進化的に仕上げていくというイメージです。

　最初の Contents の Phase では、演劇でいうならばプロットにあたる structure（構成）をしっかり組み立て、それに言葉をつけて、脚本を作成するように draft（原稿）を完成させていきます。次の Visuals の Phase では、演劇で演出効果や衣装など舞台美術面を充実させるように、画像を活かしたスライド作成により Visuals 面でも「見せる・魅せる」プレゼンテーションを目指していきます。さらに Delivery の Phase では、役者がセリフを話すように、メッセージが伝わるようなスピーチの練習を行います。その際、立ち稽古のように実際に立ち上がってオーディエンスを意識しながら自然な姿勢や体の動きが備わるように発表します。最後の Phase は、オーディエンスとの Interaction（交流）です。観客なしの演劇が存在しないように、オーディエンスのいないプレゼンテーションはありえません。オーディエンスと視線を交わし feedback を活かしながら、意味のあるやり取りを目指してください。

　各 Unit では、Key Point（学習項目）を理解し、その練習問題である Tasks を実践することにより、プレゼンテーションのスキル（技能）を習得していき、さらに Mini-Presentation でそのスキルを実践していきます。全 Unit を学習することで、あらゆる内容のプレゼンテーションに共通するスキルを一通り体得できます。また、各 Unit でのスキル学習に加え、学期末・学年末の最終プレゼンテーションに向けた準備段階が用意されています。各 Phase の後にある Mission は最終プレゼンテーションのための準備の章です。この Mission 1 〜 3 に取り組むことで、トピック選択というゼロの段階からプレゼンテーションを立ち上げ、脚本家、演出家、演者、舞台監督として 1 人何役もこなすプレゼンターターの Missions を達成させましょう。

著者一同

■ 本書の構成と特徴

　プレゼンテーションに必要なスキルを、4 Phases（Contents, Visuals, Delivery, Interaction）という段階を追って無理なく効果的に学習します。さらに、Warm-up, Key Point, Task, Mini-Presentation などを使って、「読む、聞く、書く、話す」という 4 技能上達のための練習を行い、Key Expressions で語彙力や構文力も養います。

■ 各 Phase について

Phase 1. Contents（プレゼンテーション原稿の考案と作成）Unit 1, 2, 3
Phase 2. Visuals（写真・イラスト・図表など視覚情報の提示）Unit 4, 5, 6
Phase 3. Delivery（流暢さ・ジェスチャーなどのパフォーマンスを含むメッセージの伝達）Unit 7, 8, 9
Phase 4. Interaction（オーディエンスや司会者との交流、最終プレゼンテーションのためのリハーサルと本番の心構え）Unit 10, 11, 12

■ 各 Unit の構成

各 Unit ではプレゼンテーションに重要なスキルを次のような順序で学習します。

1. You will learn：学習目標として、これから何を学習するのか確認します。
2. Warm-up：Unit の始めに、本題に入る前の予備知識をつけ、関連するトピックやスキルを学習するための準備をします。
3. Key Point：プレゼンテーションのスキルに関する具体的な学習項目です。日本語によるスキルの説明を理解した後、Task によりスキルを使いこなす練習をします。
4. Key Expressions：プレゼンテーションに必要な重要表現です。例文を音声で聴いた後、暗記できるまで音読練習するのが効果的です。
5. Give It a Try!（Mini-Presentation）：Unit の最後に、Model の話題に沿って自分だけのオリジナルのプレゼンテーションを作成し、実践します。

   Model (presentation)：1 回の授業の最後に仕上げられるような Mini-Presentation のモデルになる英文です。音声を聞いて、音読練習ができます。

   Presentation Template：Mini-Presentation 原稿の雛型です。Model を参考にして、下線部に自分の意見や情報を付け加えて、独自の原稿を作成します。
6. Check (☑) what you have learned：最初の You will learn で掲げた目標を達成できているかを章の最後で振り返り、自己点検します。

■ Mission と Optional Unit

Mission 1 〜 3：学期末・学年末に行う Final Presentation に向けての準備コーナーです。Phase 内の Units で学習した知識やスキルを統合して取り組みます。

Optional Unit：Poster presentation や Web conferencing services, tablet or smartphone presentation など専門科目の発表や卒業後に企業や学会発表などで体験することが想定されるプレゼンテーションについて学びます。

Table of Contents

Pre-Unit   What Is a Presentation? ·············· 6

Phase 1: Contents
Unit 1   Presentation Structure ················· 13
Unit 2   Informative-style Presentation ············· 19
Unit 3   Persuasive-style Presentation ············· 27
Mission ①   Write a Draft of Your Presentation! ············· 36

Phase 2: Visuals
Unit 4   Making Effective Slides ············· 40
Unit 5   Visualizing Textual Information ············· 48
Unit 6   Visualizing Quantitative Data ············· 54
Mission ②   Make Slides for Your Presentation! ············· 61

Phase 3: Delivery
Unit 7   Pronunciation Focus ············· 64
Unit 8   Telling Delivery ············· 71
Unit 9   Non-verbal Communication ············· 77
Mission ③   Deliver Your Presentation! ············· 84

Phase 4: Interaction
Unit 10   Q&A Session Strategies ············· 88
Unit 11   Rehearsal and Practice ············· 95
Unit 12   Final Presentation ············· 101

Optional Unit   Various Presentations ············· 108

Pre-Unit What Is a Presentation?

You will learn:

1. what a presentation is and what the four main phases of a presentation are
2. basics of English pronunciation (phonics & rhythm pattern of English)
3. how to share information with each other and introduce your friends

Warm-up

Have you ever given a presentation? If so, what points did you pay particular attention to? If not, what points do you think you should keep in mind?

Checklist for Presentation

Go through the following Checklist and check (✓) "what I know."

	Item	Target Phase	Unit
☐	1. How to organize your ideas into a presentation	Contents	Unit 1, 2, & 3
☐	2. How to start and close a presentation	Introduction & Conclusion	Unit 1
☐	3. How to develop your ideas within and between paragraphs	Body	Unit 2 & 3
☐	4. How to move smoothly from a main point to another main point	Transition	Unit 2 & 3
☐	5. How to use presentation tools such as PowerPoint	Visuals	Unit 4, 5, & 6
☐	6. How to create and explain infographics such as graphs or charts	Visuals	Unit 4, 5, & 6
☐	7. How to keep your audience engaged and interested	Contents, Visuals, & Delivery	Unit 1, 2, 3, 4, 5, 6, 7, 8, & 9
☐	8. How to make your presentation sound convincing	Delivery	Unit 7, 8, & 9
☐	9. How to use non-verbal language	Non-verbal Communication	Unit 9
☐	10. How to ask and answer questions	Interaction: Q&A	Unit 10

If you didn't tick on most or all of the above items, don't worry! This textbook will help you learn presentation skills step by step. Before that, try to think what a presentation is all about.

What Is a Presentation?

A presentation is the act of presenting and delivering your opinions, ideas, and information to a group of listeners called the audience. The key to success is to convince the audience of the value of your message. To make your presentation effective and successful, it is important to learn and take into consideration the following four phases: contents, visuals, delivery, and interaction with the audience.

As shown in the diagram below, each phase of the presentation plays an indispensable role in making your presentation successful.

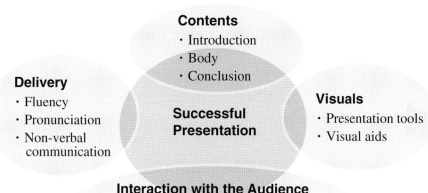

Contents

contents（内容）とは、あなたのメッセージが何であるか、あるいはオーディエンスに伝えたいことは何かということです。メッセージを効果的かつ論理的に伝達するために、プレゼンテーションは introduction（導入部・序論）、body（本論）、conclusion（結論）という 3 部から構成される明確な構造で展開される必要があります。また、トピックに応じて、情報伝達型や説得型など、さまざまなプレゼンテーションのスタイルやタイプを学習します。

Visuals

visuals（ビジュアル）とは、PowerPoint や Google Slides などのプレゼンテーションツールを使い、言葉によるメッセージを視覚化することです。"A picture is worth a thousand words." "Seeing is believing." と言われていますように視覚情報には絶大な力がありますが、ただ、写真やイラストをスライドに掲載するだけでなく、どのように見せると魅力的か、口頭説明という聴覚情報と視覚情報をどのように組み合わせればいいかという視点から効果的な提示方法を学習します。さらに、データ情報のグラフ化とわかりやすい説明方法についても学習します。

Delivery

delivery（デリバリー）とは、口頭で伝えるメッセージの明瞭さ、流暢さ、わかりやすさのことです。

具体的には、単語の発音、stress（強勢）、intonation（文の抑揚）などの音声特徴が重要な要素です。さらに、言語的（verbal）側面にとどまらず、eye contact（視線）、posture（姿勢）、gestures（身振り）などの非言語的（non-verbal）側面も充実させて、生き生きとしたプレゼンテーションを目指しましょう。

Interaction with the Audience

プレゼンテーションにはオーディエンスとの双方向のコミュニケーションが必要です。オーディエンスに質問を投げかけたり、オーディエンスからの質問に答えたりすることにより、オーディエンスとの interaction（交流）が生まれます。

さらに、近年プレゼンテーションは、poster presentation や Zoom presentation など、さまざまな形態で行われ、コミュニケーションスタイルも多様になっていますが、どんなメディアを使うにしても、プレゼンターは "for the benefit of the audience"（オーディエンスのために）を念頭に置いてオーディエンスとのやり取りを楽しみましょう。

Key Point 1 Phonics

効果的にプレゼンテーションの原稿を読むために、適切な発音を身につけましょう。phonics（フォニックス）とは、英語の綴り字と発音との間の規則性（ルール）を学ぶことですが、英語の場合、綴りと発音にはいつも 1 対 1 の関係があるとは限りません。例えば、英単語に含まれる "a" の綴りには以下のようにさまざまな発音があります。

例："a" の綴りに含まれる発音

　　/ə/: **another**　/e/: **any**　/æ/: **relax**　/ɑːr/: **far**　/ɔː/: **talk**　/eɪ/: **make**

Task 1 Phonics Game

Find and circle the words in the following table that are pronounced /eɪ/. Move across or down. Do not move diagonally. Do not skip words. Then add an arrow (→) to show the direction.

START			
made	mad	math	chance
maid	male	mat	matter
said	May	eight	height
sad	any	freight	say
man	many	seal	sail
tall	tell	tail	sale
talk	treat	great	greet
tally	letter	late	latter
variety	apply	April	make
			FINISH

Task 2 Phonics Rule

Fill in the blanks in the following table using the words in Task 1. Compare your answers in pairs.

Spelling pronounced as /eɪ/	Word
Words with the spelling "a"	made ( ) ( ) ( ) ( ) ( )
Words with the spelling "ai"	( ) ( ) ( )
Words with the spelling "ay"	( ) ( )
Words with the spelling "ei"	( ) ( )
Words with the spelling "ea"	( )

Key Point 2 Rhythm Pattern of English　🎧 03

1. 英語では、一般的に①**内容語 (content words)** は強く、②**機能語 (function words)** は通常、弱く発音されます。

　①内容語：それ自体が意味を持つ語（例：名詞、動詞、副詞、形容詞、疑問詞など）

　②機能語：日本語の助詞のように、文中で内容語を補助する語（例：be動詞、人称代名詞、前置詞、冠詞など）

2. 音節 (syllables) とは母音を1つ含む音の区切りです。多音節から構成される内容語には、1つの語の中で強く読む強音節 (●) と弱く読む弱音節 (○) があります。

　例： pre-sen-ta-tion
　　　　○　○　●　○

3. 英語には弱く発音する弱音節と強く発音する強音節が交互に現れるリズム構造があり、戯曲や詩のような文学作品だけでなく、日常的に使われています。弱強（○ ●）が基本のリズムですが、前置詞や冠詞が続くことも多いことから、弱弱（○○）が続いたり、内容語が続くとき、強強（● ●）が続いたりすることもあります。

　例： I **think** they're **great** com**po**sers.（日常会話）
　　　 ○ ● 　○ ○ ● 　○ ● ○

　　　 I'll **tra**vel in **France next sum**mer.（日常会話）
　　　 ○ ● ○ ○ 　● 　　● ● ○

　　　 I **went** to Aus**tra**lia with my **un**cle **last Au**gust.（日常会話）
　　　 ○ ● ○ ○ ● ○ 　○ 　○ ● 　　● ● ○

　　　 To **be**, or **not** to **be**, **that** is the **ques**tion. (*Hamlet*, William Shakespeare)
　　　 ○ ● ○ ● ○ ● 　● 　○ ○ 　● 　○

Task 3　Pronunciation Practice (Mother Goose)

Repeat after the audio, paying attention to stressed syllables.

Humpty **Dum**pty **sat** on a **wall**,
● ○ ● ○ ● ○○ ●

Humpty **Dum**pty **had** a **great fall**;
● ○ ● ○ ● ○ ● ●

All the **king's horse**es and **all** the **king's men**
● ○ ● ● ○○ ● ○ ● ●

Couldn't **put Hum**pty to**ge**ther a**gain**.
● ● ● ○○● ○ ○ ●

Key Point 3　Making Friends with Your Classmates

プレゼンテーションの一番の基本である自己紹介（self-introduction）、友人など他の人を紹介する仕方を学習します。自己紹介も他の人物紹介も基本的には同じですが、人称代名詞や３人称単数現在形のように動詞の活用にも気をつけて、自然に発話できるように練習しましょう。人物紹介ができれば司会（moderator）も務めることができます。

Key Expressions

■ Expressions for Getting to Know Each Other Better

1. **Do you like** sports / music / movies?　**Are you interested in** sports / music / movies?
   Yes ⇒ What kind of sports / music / movies do you like?
   　　 ⇒ Who is your favorite athlete / musician / artist / movie star?
   No　⇒ What do you like to do in your free time?（*Change the topic*）

2. **Are you a member of** a tennis club / an orchestra club / a drama club?
   Yes ⇒ How often do you practice?
   No　⇒ What do you like to do after school?（*Change the topic*）

3. **Do you work part-time**?
   Yes ⇒ How often do you work part-time?
   No　⇒ What do you like to do after school?（*Change the topic*）

4. **Do you like** traveling / watching sports / listening to music?
   Yes ⇒ Have you ever traveled abroad?
   No　⇒ What are you planning to do next summer?（*Change the topic*）
   Yes ⇒ What country do you like best?

Task 4　Information-Sharing with Your Classmates

Ask classmates the following questions and complete the table below.

Start by saying "Hello" to your classmate. For example, "Hi! I'm (*your name*). Nice to meet you," if you are meeting him or her for the first time.

After that, share information with your classmates, using the question-answer pattern below.

1. **Name**

   Q: Can I ask your name? / May I have your name, please? (*formal*)

   A: My name is / I'm _____. Please call me _____.

2. **Major**

   Q: What is your major?

   A: My major is / I major in _____.

3. **Favorite music**

   Q: Do you like music? What kind of music do you like?

   A: I like _____ (very much), (especially) _____.

4. **Favorite movies**

   Q: Do you like movies? What kind of movies do you like?

   A: I like _____ movies. My favorite actor / actress is _____.

5. **Club (Extracurricular activities)**

   Q: Are you a member of any club?

   A: Yes. I'm a member of _____.

6. **Part-time job**

   Q: Do you work part-time after school?

   A: Yes. I work as a _____ on weekends.

1. Name	2. Major	3. Favorite music	4. Favorite movie	5. Club	6. Part-time job	7. Other information
SATO Kana	Psychology	J-pop Yumin	romantic movie Julia Roberts	tennis twice/week	tutor weekend	

<u>Give It a Try!</u>　Mini-Presentation

Based on the Model, fill in the blanks of the Presentation Template, and give a presentation about introducing your classmate.

Hello, everyone. My name is Shiori Maki. **Let me introduce** my classmate / friend, Ms. Kana Sato. She **is majoring in** psychology. Her **favorite subjects are** mathematics, computer science, and English. So she **is taking** the data science and statistics **courses.** She **likes** many kinds of sports, including figure skating. Her **favorite athlete is** Yuzuru Hanyu. She also likes listening to J-pop. **When it comes to movies,** she **is interested in** romantic movies and her **favorite** movie star **is** Julia Roberts. She **belongs to** a tennis club and **practices** twice a week. She **is working part-time as** a tutor **on weekends.** She says she would like to make as many friends as possible. When you talk to her, you'll find her very cheerful and friendly.

Presentation Template

Hello, everyone. My name is _____.

Let me introduce my classmate / friend, Mr. / Ms. _____.

He / She is majoring in _____.

His / Her favorite subjects are _____.

He / She is taking _____ courses.

He / She likes _____.

His / Her favorite athlete / artist / movie star is _____.

He / She is interested in _____.

He / She belongs to / is a member of _____ club and

practices _____ a week.

He / She is working part-time as a _____ on weekends.

Check (☑) what you have learned:

☐	what a presentation is and what the four main phases of a presentation are
☐	basics of English pronunciation (phonics & rhythm pattern of English)
☐	how to share information with each other and introduce friends

Unit 1 Presentation Structure

You will learn:

1. presentation structure
2. elements of 'Introduction' & 'Conclusion'
3. organization of 'Introduction' & 'Conclusion'

Warm-up

Learn the structure of a presentation. Then, fill in the blanks.

A presentation is divided into three main parts: Introduction, Body, and Conclusion. 'The Introduction' is the very first part of presentation, so it should capture the audience's interest, introduce the background information, state your thesis statement*, and outline the flow of your presentation. 'The Body' constitutes several paragraphs, providing facts, examples, and evidence to support the thesis statement shown in the Introduction. Each paragraph has a single main idea, which is in the topic sentence often located at the beginning of the paragraph. 'The Conclusion,' which follows the Body, usually includes a restatement of the thesis and brief summary of your arguments. Thus, the Introduction and Conclusion are quite similar in content.

(^{1})	: background, thesis statement, outline, etc.
(Body)	: several paragraphs to support thesis statement
(^{2})	: restatement of thesis statement, brief summary, etc.

* thesis statement: statement of your point of view on the topic, usually a single sentence near the beginning of the introduction that presents your argument to the audience. In other words, it tells the audience what to expect from the rest of the presentation.

Key Point 1   Contents of Introduction and Conclusion

プレゼンテーションにおける Introduction は「これから何を述べるのか」といった、その目的を知らせる導入部分です。背景情報、あなたの主張や発表全体のアウトラインだけでなく、オーディエンスの興味を惹きつける引用などを含めるといいでしょう。一方、最後のパラグラフである Conclusion では「これまで何を述べてきたか」をまとめる部分であり、何を伝えたかったのかを再確認し結論を提示する部分でもあります。そのため、Conclusion は内容的に Introduction と共通点があります。また今後の展望や課題・提案などを含めるのもいいでしょう。

Task 1 Consider whether the next items should be included in the 'Introduction' or the 'Conclusion'.

1. トピックの概要 （　　　　　）
2. 問題の解決策へのコメント （　　　　　）
3. ことわざや逸話 （　　　　　）
4. 提案や今後の課題・展望 （　　　　　）
5. トピックに関した引用 （　　　　　）
6. 使用する言葉や略語の定義・説明 （　　　　　）
7. 結論や結果 （　　　　　）
8. 問題の背景や現状 （　　　　　）

Key Point 2 How to Organize Your Introduction

Introduction は、司会者（moderator）への感謝やオーディエンスへの挨拶、自己紹介から始まります。ここでは発表のテーマや目的、次にそれに関する一般的な背景情報を紹介し、引用や軽い問いかけなどを含めてオーディエンスの興味を惹くこともあります。最後に自分の発表のポイントへと絞り込み、発表内容の概要（outline）をまとめます。つまり general な情報からあなた独自の specific な発表、特定の情報へと絞り込む「逆三角形」のイメージで作成しましょう。

general

specific

上のイメージを箇条書きにしてみます。

Introduction: general（一般的な情報）→ specific（特定の情報）

1. 司会者への感謝やオーディエンスへの挨拶、自己紹介
2. 発表のテーマや目的
3. テーマに関する一般的な背景情報
4. ことわざや有名な文章の引用や軽い問いかけ（もしあれば）
5. 発表内容の概要

Task 2　Put the information below in the right order.

a) outline of the presentation　　b) background information

c) greeting & opening remarks　　d) purpose of the presentation

(¹　　　) ➡ (²　　　) ➡ (³　　　) ➡ (⁴　　　)

Key Point 3　How to Organize Your Conclusion

Conclusion は、あなたの発表の要約や結論を述べ、最後の挨拶や清聴への感謝を示して締めくくる部分ですが、あなたの発表でオーディエンスが「何を知りえたか」をまとめて提示する機会でもあります。それゆえあなたの発表を自分独自のものから、オーディエンスにも役立つように一般化していくことが大事です。トピックに関する今後の予測や展望、オーディエンスへの提案や推奨事項を述べることが多いのはそのためです。つまりあなた独自の specific な結論から汎用性のある general な情報へと拡大していく「三角形」のイメージで作成しましょう。

specific

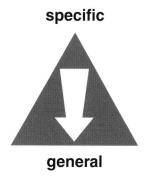

general

こちらのイメージも箇条書きにしてみます。

Conclusion: specific（あなた独自の結論）→ general（汎用性のある結論）

1. 発表の要約や結論
2. 結論に関する今後の予測や展望、提案
3. 結びの言葉
4. 清聴への感謝

Task 3　Put the information below in the right order.

a) conclusion of the presentation　　b) appreciation for attention

c) closing remarks　　d) future challenges and prospects

(¹　　　) ➡ (²　　　) ➡ (³　　　) ➡ (⁴　　　)

Key Expressions

■ Expressions for Introduction

● **The topic of my presentation today is** "Preventing Elderly Driver Accidents."
今日の私の発表テーマは「高齢者ドライバーの事故防止」です。

● **I'm going to give you some background information about** renewable energy in Japan.
日本の再生可能エネルギーについて背景を説明します。

● **Let me start by telling you briefly about** the present situation in sub-Saharan countries.　まず、サハラ砂漠以南の諸国の現状について簡単にお話しします。

● **Here is the outline of my presentation.**　発表の概要は以下の通りです。

■ Expressions for Conclusion

● **So far, I have explained to you** the importance of SDGs.
これまで、SDGs の重要性をご説明してきました。

● **Let me summarize the points.**　ポイントを整理してみます。

● **For these reasons**, I'm willing to work with A.I. robots.
以上の理由から、私はよろこんで AI ロボットと協業します。

● **As I stated earlier**, renewable energy is safe and clean.
先ほども申し上げたように、再生可能エネルギーは安全でクリーンなものです。

● **In conclusion**, I think we should abandon the use of fossil fuels.
結論として、化石エネルギーの利用を断念すべきだと思います。

● **Thank you for your kind attention.**　ご清聴ありがとうございました。

Give It a Try! Mini-Presentation

Based on the Model, give a presentation using the Presentation Template below.

Model Introduction を読んで、Task 2 で学んだ Introduction の構成要素を確認しましょう。

Model Social Media and Personal Relationships 08

> **Thank you very much, Professor Jones. Hello, everyone! I'm** Ken Yamamoto **from** Powerful **University**. **Today, I'd like to talk about** 'Social Media and Personal Relationships.' Since we are digital natives, our smartphone is almost a part of our body, isn't it? I can't imagine a day without checking social media. But at the same time, these services can also hurt people if not used carefully and appropriately. **So, first I will explain the background of** current social media and describe the advantages and disadvantages of social networking. **After that, I will explore** the harmful effects the wrongful use of social media can have on personal relationships. **Finally, I will** try to show you the ideal relationship between social media and us.

Task 4

1. Classify and underline each of the parts corresponding to a) the outline of the presentation, b) the background of the topic, c) the greeting & opening remarks, and d) the purpose of the presentation.

2. In pairs, practice reading aloud until you can read it smoothly.

Task 5

1. Choose a topic from the alternatives below. Based on the model, give a presentation, using the presentation template below.

   alternatives:
   <Gender Gap in Japan>   <The Dark Side of Pet Shops>
   <Remote vs Face-to-Face Classes>   <Human Coexistence with A.I. Robots>
   <Dos & Don'ts When Traveling Abroad>

Presentation Template

Thank you very much, Mr./Ms. XX. Hello, everyone. I'm _____ from _____ University. Today, I'd like to talk about _____ _____ _____.

So, first I will explain the background of _____ _____.

After that, I will explore _____.
_____.

Finally, I will _____
_____.

2. In groups, present your 'Introduction' and give peer-feedback to each other.

❗ Presentation Tips

プレゼンテーションを行う際に最も緊張するのは Introduction、つまりオーディエンスの注目を一身に浴びる最初のオープニング部分と言ってもいいでしょう。PowerPoint を使用した発表の場合なら、Body 部分が始まればオーディエンスの注目はスライドに注がれますので、あなたも落ち着いて発表に集中することができます。ここをうまく乗り切って効果的なプレゼンテーションにしましょう！

Check (☑) what you have learned:

☐	the structure of a presentation
☐	the elements of 'Introduction' & 'Conclusion'
☐	how to organize 'Introduction' & 'Conclusion'

Unit 2　Informative-style Presentation

You will learn:

1. the features of two types of an informative-style presentation
2. the structure of two types of an informative-style presentation
3. how to arrange and organize information and messages into presentation structure

Warm-up

An informative-style presentation is intended to convey the presenter's knowledge of a particular topic to an audience through explanation, description, and/or demonstration. The way the information is presented can mainly take two forms: "listing" type and "procedural" type. The former features information listed in an item-by-item way. Information is grouped, with each group labeled, according to its most important feature. The latter features information presented in a sequential manner. Its aim is to explain the step-by-step procedures, such as a recipe.

Based on the explanation above, categorize the following topics into "listing" type (L) and "procedural" type (P).

1. What are the secrets of successful companies?　2. How to solve food loss
3. How to operate a PC　4. Top 20 most popular fruits in Japan
5. How to promote SDGs　6. The features of the latest robots
7. Top 10 best global companies ranking

Key Point 1　What is the Body?

body（本論）は プレゼンテーションの中核を構成し、実質的な内容を伝達する重要な部分です。情報内容によって以下のように分類されます。

1. informative-style presentation（情報伝達型プレゼンテーション）
   情報や知識を伝達するプレゼンテーション
   (1) listing-type presentation（情報列挙型プレゼンテーション）
   (2) procedural-type presentation（手続き説明型プレゼンテーション）
2. persuasive-style presentation（説得型プレゼンテーション）Unit 3参照

どのスタイル、タイプのプレゼンテーションであっても、body は複数の段落から構成され、それぞれの段落は 1 つの main idea と複数の supporting details から構成されます。

Main Idea: 段落の核となる情報や意見 = Topic Sentence（主題文）

　　　1st Supporting Details: Main Idea を支持する補足説明文

　　　　　　　　　Main Idea の理由付け（reasons）、証拠（evidence）、例証（examples）など

　　　Nth Supporting Details: Main Idea を支持する補足説明文（N= 数字番号）

　　　　　　　　　Main Idea の理由付け（reasons）、証拠（evidence）、例証（examples）など

原稿を書く前に、全体の structure（構成）を考えましょう。

Key Point **2**　　The Structure of Listing-type Presentation

listing-type presentation（情報列挙型プレゼンテーション）ではプレゼンターが情報の項目を列挙しながら説明します。introduction（序論）で紹介した項目を body（本論）で 1 つずつ詳細に説明します。thesis statement（主張文）は Unit 1（p. 13）参照。

Task **1**　　Convert the Presentation Sample into the Structure below. Write the Topic, Thesis Statement, and Conclusion. Fill in the brackets [ ] with appropriate statement numbers [1]~[11] of the Presentation Sample.

The Listing-type Presentation Structure

I. Introduction

   Topic: ....

   Thesis Statement: ....

II. Body

   Main Idea 1 (Item 1): .... [　　]

     Supporting Details .... [　　]

     .... [　　]

     .... [　　]

   Main Idea 2 (Item 2): .... [　　]

     Supporting Details .... [　　]

     .... [　　]

   Main Idea 3 (Item 3): .... [　　]

     Supporting Details .... [　　]

     .... [　　]

     .... [　　]

  III. Conclusion: ....

Presentation Sample

 09

Topic: The Three Effective Skills University Students Need to Develop

Thesis Statement: Students **should** develop 1. critical thinking skills, 2. PC literacy, and 3. presentation skills.

First and foremost, critical thinking skills **top the list** [1]. Critical thinking gets students making reasoned evaluations based on their understanding, analysis, and interpretation of what they have learned through reading and lectures [2]. This skill **is essential to** construct**ing** their own argument or position on various issues [3]. Whatever their discipline, students **should** develop the ability to put things into perspectives and think logically and critically [4].

Second, practically speaking, students **need to** acquire PC literacy [5]. Computers allow them not only to gather information through a search engine, but also to compose documents, make figures and tables, and summarize them in charts [6]. Furthermore, these days programming knowledge **is required** from elementary school age, so a minimum knowledge of programming **is desirable** [7].

Last, but not least, presentation skills **are of utmost importance** [8]. Presentation skills mean the ability to effectively explain the knowledge and information students want to share with the audience and to persuasively present the arguments they want to put forth [9]. **By** acquir**ing** presentation skills, students **can** learn how to communicate their ideas logically and to interact verbally and non-verbally with their audience [10]. So presentation skills **are one of the most important** communication **skills** they **need to** develop through their study of academic disciplines [11].

To sum up, these three skills will empower students to navigate their way through their university life and beyond.

Key Point 3　The Structure of Procedural-type Presentation

informative-style presentation のもう 1 つの典型例である **procedural-type presentation**（手続き説明型プレゼンテーション）ではプレゼンターが何かの仕方の手順や工程を順序よく説明します。手順以外に、歴史的事件のように情報を年代順や時系列的に説明する場合（chronological or time-order type presentation）もあります。手続き型の main ideas は steps = procedures（手順）になりますが、例えば調理法であれば、1. 材料の下ごしらえ、2. 材料の焼き方・炒め方等のように、情報をグループ化してまとめて提示します。

Task 2 Convert the Presentation Sample into the Structure below. Fill in the blanks (   ). Filll in the brackets [ ] with appropriate statement numbers [1]~[20] of the Presentation Sample.

The Procedural-type Presentation Structure

I. Introduction

    Topic: How to make (   ) food

II. Body

    1. The 1st Group of Steps: how to make (   ) .... [   ]

      Step 1 .... [   ]

      Step 2 .... [   ]

      Step 3 .... [   ]

    2. The 2nd Group of Steps: how to prepare (   ) .... [   ]

      Step 1 .... [   ]

      Step 2 .... [   ]

      Step 3 .... [   ]

    3. The 3rd Group of Steps: how to prepare (   ) .... [   ]

      Step 1 .... [   ]

      Step 2 .... [   ]

    4. The 4th Group of Steps: how to (   ) the ingredients .... [   ]

      Step 1 .... [   ]

      Step 2 .... [   ]

      Step 3 .... [   ]

      Step 4 .... [   ]

III. Closing

    Remarks & Additional Information (if any): useful (   ) .... [   ]

    .... [   ]

    .... [   ]

    .... [   ]

Presentation Sample　　　　　　　　　　　🎧 10

How to Make Tempura (Deep-fried Food)

(After introducing the topic and explaining the ingredients needed …,)

　　First, I will show you how to make batter, the mixture of flour, egg, and, water [1]. Crack the eggs into a bowl and beat well [2]. Pour ice-cold water into the bowl [3]. Then sift the flour into the egg mixture and mix with chopsticks well until no lumps remain [4]. *So far, I have explained how to make Tempura batter.* Then, shall we prepare the ingredients?**

　　Next, let me show how to prepare prawn or shrimp, one of the most-favored ingredients for tempura [5]. Pull off the outer shell and devein the prawns [6]. Leave the last segment of shell and the tail tip intact [7]. Furthermore, make four or five shallow cuts on the belly side to prevent them from curling up when fried [8].

　　Third, I will show you how to prepare the vegetables [9]. Slice the vegetables such as pumpkin and sweet potato thinly [10]. Cut the eggplants into quarters [11]. *Okay?***

　　Now it's time to demonstrate how to deep-fry these ingredients [12]. *You see? Like this!*** Start by pouring deep-frying oil into the pot and heat to 180°C [13]. Deep-fry the seafood at 180°C [14]. Deep-fry the vegetables slowly at 160-170°C [15]. To finish up, drain off the oil when cooked through [16].

　　It's done! Got it? Easy, isn't it?** *(response from the audience)* I'd like to add some useful tips [17]. To make tasty tempura, vary the frying temperature and time according to the ingredients [18]. Do not use too many ingredients at the same time [19]. In addition, mix a small amount of sesame oil if available with vegetable oil to create crispy texture [20].

---

*transition を表す表現　Key Point 4 参照　　** オーディエンスが理解しているかチェックする表現

Key Point 4　　What Is the Transition?

プレゼンテーションで、1つの main idea から次の main idea に移行することを示す signposting（道標、道しるべ）を示すと聞き手が理解しやすくなります。signposting expressions となる transition には conjunctions（接続詞）と transitional phrases（アイディアを繋ぐ言葉）があります。

Conjunctions

順序→ before this, first, second, then, next, afterwards, etc.

追加→ and, also, in addition, additionally, moreover, furthermore, etc.

逆説→ but, however, even so, though, nevertheless, nonetheless, still, yet, in contrast, on the other hand, on the contrary, etc.

理由→ because. this is because

結果→ so, therefore, consequently, for this reason, as a result, that is why,

Transitional Phrases

プレゼンテーションの構造上、Main Idea 1 等、あるセクションを終了させるとき

- (Up to now,) I've looked at ....
- (So far,) I've talked about ....

Main Idea1 の後、新情報 Main Idea 2 などを始めるとき

- Let me move on to ....
- Now, let's turn to ....
- And I'd now like to talk about ....
- The next / second ....
- I'd now like to explain ....
- The next issue/topic/area I'd like to focus on is ....

Conclusion を導くとき

- To sum up, / To summarize, ...
- I'd now like to summarize ....
- So, from what we have discussed today, we can say that ....

Task 3 Read the two Presentation Samples above: "The Three Effective Skills University Students Need to Develop" and "How to Make Tempura." <u>Underline</u> the conjunctions and transitional phrases.

Key Expressions   🎧 11

■ Expressions for Explaining the List of Items

- **I will explain characteristic features of** this new device **one by one**.
  この新しい機器の特徴を一つ一つ説明いたします。
- **First and foremost,** convenient functions are added to the conventional one.
  まず、第1に、便利な機能が従来品に付け加えられています。
- **Second / Secondly,** the product is more lightweight.
  2番目に、本製品はより軽量化しています。
- **Third / Thirdly,** prices are reduced considerably.
  3番目に、価格がかなり抑えられています。
- **Finally, / Last, but not least,** the product is more cost-effective than the earlier version.
  最後に / 最後になりましたが、重要なこととして、本製品は従来品と比較して、より費用対効果の高い製品になっています。

■ Expressions for Stating the Purpose of the Presentation

- **After listening to this talk, you will find it easy and enjoyable to** use this smartphone.　この話を聞けばこのスマホを使うことは簡単で楽しいことがわかります。
- **This explanation will help you** understand the value of SDGs better.
  この説明を聞けば SDG の価値をより良く理解できるでしょう。

24

- **Please follow these procedures, and you will be able to** register on your own.
  この手続きを踏んでください。そうすれば自分で登録できるでしょう。

■ Expressions for Explaining Procedures

- **I will show you how to make** an omelet.　オムレツの作り方を実演します。
- **Start by** preparing the vegetables.　まず、野菜を準備します。
- **Up to now, I have explained how to** gather information.
  これまで、情報の収集方法について説明しました。
- **Next, I will explain how to** organize information.
  次に、情報の整理方法を説明いたします。

Give It a Try!　Mini-Presentation

Introduce the recipe of your favorite food. Based on the Model, give a presentation using the Presentation Template below.

Model (Procedural-type Presentation)　The Recipe of *Nikujaga* 12

> **I'm going to show you how to** make *nikujaga,* or cooked meat and vegetables.
>
> **After listening to the steps, you will find** it easy and enjoyable to make tasty *nikujaga*.
>
> **First, I will show you how to** prepare ingredients. Cut vegetables such as an onion, carrots, peeled potatoes into bite-sized pieces.
>
> **Second, let me show how to** cook these ingredients. **Start by** cook**ing** the onion in a large pot. **Next,** add thinly sliced meat (beef or pork).
>
> **After that,** add the rest of the ingredients, including cooked *shirataki* noodles.
>
> **Finally,** add seasoning such as soy sauce, sugar, and rice wine. Simmer the ingredients for about 15 minutes.

Presentation Template (Procedural-type Presentation)

> I'm going to show you how to _____.
>
> After listening to the steps, you will find _____.
>
> First, I will show you how to _____.
>
> Second, let me show how to _____.
>
> Start by _____.

Next, _____ .

After that, _____ .

Finally, _____ .

参考 Checklist

draft（原稿）を書き終わったら informative-style presentation（情報伝達型プレゼンテーション）の body（本論）の部分を次の checklist に照らし合わせて点検し、推敲しましょう。

Content（内容）

☐ Are the topic, the thesis statement, and main ideas clear and understandable?

☐ Is the information accurate and understandable?

☐ Is the information interesting enough to arouse the audience's interests?

☐ Is the information well-focused and well-organized?

Structure（構成）

☐ Are the body paragraphs clearly focused on the topic or the thesis statement described in the introduction?

☐ Are the main ideas effectively supported by reasoning, examples, and/or evidence?

☐ Does the presenter use conjunctions and transitional phrases effectively?

☐ Does the conclusion summarize the main ideas/points of the body?

Editing（編集）

☐ Does the presenter run spellcheck, and redress grammatical or word errors (e.g., verb tense errors, subject-verb agreement errors) thoroughly after writing the first draft?

☐ Are there errors that alter the meaning of the text or make the message unclear?

Check (☑) what you have learned:

☐	the features of two types of an informative-style presentation
☐	the structure of two types of an informative-style presentation
☐	how to arrange and organize information and messages into presentation structure

Unit 3　Persuasive-style Presentation

You will learn:

1. the features of two types of a persuasive-style presentation
2. the structure of two types of a persuasive-style presentation
3. how to organize and develop a standpoint

Warm-up

A persuasive-style presentation presents a presenter's stance on a particular issue, on which he or she mostly states affirmative or negative views. Among a variety of forms this style of presentation can take, the "opinion-building" and "problem-solving" types are common. The first type features the presenter's opinion over a particular issue, which is supported by reasons and evidence. The reasons should be compelling enough to persuade the audience. The second type begins with the statement of a problem. After giving its causes and explaining its seriousness, the presenter gives what he or she thinks are the best solutions.

Based on the explanation above, categorize the following topics into "opinion-building" type (O) and "problem-solving" type (P).

1. How to save endangered species
2. The significance of studying abroad
3. How to improve English proficiency
4. Students should wear uniforms
5. Which is better, paper book or e-book?
6. How to stop deforestation

Persuasive-style Presentation（説得型プレゼンテーション）
説得型プレゼンテーションは議論の展開方法により次の2つに分類されます。
　（1）opinion-building type presentation（意見提示型プレゼンテーション）
　（2）problem-solving type presentation（問題解決型プレゼンテーション）
この章では presentation structure のうちの body（本論）の書き方を中心に展開します。

Key Point 1　The Structure of Opinion-building Type Presentation

opinion-building type presentation（意見提示型プレゼンテーション）では、プレゼンターがある問題や現状に対して自身の意見、特に賛成論か反対論を述べ、主張を裏付ける理由やエビデンスを挙げ、聴衆を説得します。

27

Introduction: 問題とその定義、深刻さの程度、背景情報などを説明する

    Thesis Statement: 問題に対するプレゼンターの主張、意見を述べる

Body: 主張について理由やエビデンスを述べる

Conclusion: 主張についての反論 (counter-argument) を一部紹介し、それを打ち消しながら問題と解決策を強調してまとめる

Task 1   Convert the Presentation Sample into the Structure below. Write the Topic and Thesis statement. Fill in the brackets [ ] with appropriate statement numbers [1]~[12] of Presentation Sample.

The Opinion-building Type Presentation Structure

I. Introduction

  Topic: ....

  Thesis Statement: ....

II. Body

  Reason 1 .... [   ]

    Supporting Details .... [   ][   ]

  Reason 2 .... [   ]

    Supporting Details .... [   ][   ]

  Reason 3 .... [   ]

    Supporting Details .... [   ][   ]

III. Conclusion

  Summary .... [   ]

  Rephrasing & Emphasizing the Thesis Statement

    .... [   ]

    .... [   ]

Presentation Sample

🎧 13

Topic: Why We Should Not Give Children a Smartphone

Thesis Statement: Children **should** not be given a smartphone for the three reasons.

    Firstly, although a smartphone can allow children access to a vast amount of information through the Internet, children can be swept away by the flood of information

[1]. **More seriously,** most information coming from the Internet is neither carefully examined nor checked for accuracy [2]. Children cannot make informed judgements over which information is correct or not, even if it is fake, biased, or taken from unreliable sources [3].

Secondly, smartphones **can cause** children physical **problems** [4]. Children tend to become addicted to computer games, with their eyes continuously glued to the screen [5]. Blue light coming from the screen **is harmful to** their eyesight and exposure to the screen before bedtime **may deprive** them **of** good sleep [6].

Finally, smartphones **are not good for** their mental health [7]. Smartphone-addicted children cannot focus their attention on study during class time [8]. **To make matters worse,** addiction to games and animation **may hamper** their imagination and critical thinking skills, which could be fostered through reading good books [9].

To summarize, smartphones **cause** children **various problems** [10]. Although smartphones can give them access to educationally useful apps, **the disadvantages far outweigh the advantages** [11]. **Therefore,** if parents sincerely hope for their children's healthy growth both mentally and physically, they **should** not buy their children a smartphone [12].

Key Point 2   The Structure of Problem-solving Type Presentation

problem-solving type presentation（問題解決型プレゼンテーション）では、プレゼンターが問題とその背景を述べ、その深刻さの程度や原因を説明した後で、解決法を提示します。問題の解決法は複数の場合もあり、どれも実行可能性のある（feasible）、現実的な（realistic）案にする必要があります。解決法の利点（advantages）を強調するとさらに説得力があります。

Introduction: 問題とその定義、深刻さの程度、背景情報などを説明する

     Thesis Statement: 問題は以下の方法で解決すべきである

Body: 解決策を利点中心に詳しく説明する

Conclusion: 解決策についての反論（counter-argument）を一部紹介し、それを打ち消しながら問題と解決策を強調してまとめる

....

Task 2   Convert the Presentation Sample into the Structure below. Fill in the brackets [ ] with appropriate statement numbers [1]~[28] of Presentation Sample.

The Problem-solving Type Presentation Structure

I. Introduction

  Topic: .... [ ]

  Explanation of the Problem:

    Background of the Problem: .... [ ] [ ]

    Its Severity & Causes: .... [ ]

  Thesis Statement (Solutions): .... [ ]

II. Body

  1. Solution 1 .... [ ]

    Supporting Details: Reason .... [ ]

    Supporting Details: Solution .... [ ]

      Further detailed explanation .... [ ] [ ]

    Supporting Details: Solution .... [ ]

      Further detailed explanation .... [ ] [ ]

  2. Solution 2 .... [ ]

    Supporting Details: Solution .... [ ]

      Further detailed explanation .... [ ]

    Supporting Details: Solution .... [ ]

      Further detailed explanation .... [ ] [ ]

  3. Solution 3 .... [ ]

    Supporting Details: Reason .... [ ]

    Supporting Details: Solution .... [ ]

      Further detailed explanation .... [ ] [ ]

  III. Conclusion (Summary of the Solutions) .... [ ]

  Counter-argument .... [ ]

  Rephrasing the Thesis Statement .... [ ] [ ]

Presentation Sample

🎧 14

How to Reduce Food Loss

One of the biggest challenges facing the world today is a staggering amount of edible, but unconsumed food [1]. An estimated 931 million tons of food, accounting for 17% of total food available to consumers, were thrown out by households and food-related business operators, **according to** the United Nations Environment Programme (UNEP) [2]. Japan is no exception, where food loss and waste generated by food-related business operators and households, was estimated at more than 5.70 million tons in 2019, **according to** the Ministry of Agriculture, Forestry, and Fisheries [3]. Food loss and waste **is responsible for** greenhouse gas emissions**, thus contributing to** global climate change [4]. **Therefore, I would propose taking the following measures to** minimize the ever-increasing amount of food loss and waste [5].

First, food loss **should** be reduced at the household level [6]. Of the total amount of food loss and waste, the estimated amount of food loss and waste generated by households was 2.61 million tons in 2019 [7]. As consumers, **don't** buy more than we need [8]. Check what is available in the refrigerator and make a shopping list, **so that** we **can** avoid impulse buys and hoarding [9]. Or don't buy any food in bulk, even if it is sold at knockdown prices [10]. **Furthermore, don't** cook more than we eat [11]. **Why don't we** cook and prepare food in smaller portions, in order to avoid generating leftovers [12]**?** Or find environmentally friendly recipes, **so that** edible leftovers **could** be reused or recooked to create new dishes [13].

Second, to reduce food loss at food-related businesses **is of crucial importance** [14]. Supermarkets and grocery stores **should** keep a detailed stock inventory to track what they have in stock at all times [15]. **This will help** them avoid excess stock or orders of unwanted items [16]. **At the same time,** retailers **should** keep track of consumers' behavior, which indicates what food items tend to be left unsold [17]. Some unsold items include so-called 'ugly' non-standard vegetables or fruits, sometimes with bruises or blemishes [18]. Stores **could** mark down such items that do not meet aesthetic criteria, as well as items that are nearing the expiration date [19].

Finally, let me propose sharing how-to-avoid-food-loss information on the web [20]. Stores want to sell unsold items nearing the sell-by dates, but consumers don't know in real-time when and where such items are available [21]. **One solution is** designing an app that helps retailers redistribute discounted surplus food to cost-conscious consumers [22]. *Flashfood* or *Too Good to Go* are the examples of apps that yield win-win options for consumers who want to save money and retailers who need to sell products that are close to sell-by dates [23]. I hope such a food-rescue online network will expand to our local favorite stores and involve more food-related operators such as restaurants or eateries in our neighborhood [24].

To sum up, I have explained how serious food loss **is** and **have shared my thoughts on solutions** [25]. **Some critics doubt** small individual changes make a big difference [26]. **However,** this is another example of "think globally and act locally" [27]. **If we seriously tackle** this problem of global concern, **I'm sure we will be able to** come up with effective solutions [28].

Key Expressions

▓ Expressions for Giving an Opinion

● **I think** we **should** adopt learning about presentation skills in the classroom.
教室においてプレゼンテーションスキルの学習を取り入れる**べきだと思います**。

● **I firmly believe** we **should** separate burnable from unburnable garbage.
燃えるゴミと燃えないゴミを分別する**べきだと確信しています**。

● **In my opinion,** we **should** use bicycles to keep fit.
私の意見では、健康を維持するために自転車を使う**べきです**。

▓ Expressions for Presenting a Problem

● Littering on the street **poses a serious problem to** local residents.
道路上のごみの散らかしは住民**にとって深刻な問題になっています**。

● Overcrowded trains **result in tremendous stress to** commuters.
混雑し過ぎている電車は通勤客に**大変なストレスという結果を招いています**。

● The aging society **is becoming a serious problem.** 高齢化社会は**深刻な問題になっています**。

▓ Expressions for Presenting Causes/Reasons of the Problem

● **One of the causes of** depopulation in rural areas **is** the lack of employment opportunities.
田舎における人口減少**問題の原因の１つは**就職の機会が欠如していることです。

● **Another cause is** the inconvenience in terms of shopping and transportation.
もう１つの原因は買い物や交通の不便さです。

● The environmental **problem is mainly caused by** the increasing amount of CO_2 released into the atmosphere.
環境**問題の主な原因は**大気中に排出される二酸化炭素量の増加です。

● Declining productivity **is due to** the low level of satisfaction with work.
生産性の減少**の原因は**仕事に対する低い満足度です。

▓ Expressions for Presenting a Solution

● **One effective way of solving** the online security **problem is to** change your password frequently. ネットのセキュリティー**問題を解決するための効果的な方法の１つは**パスワードを頻繁に変えることです。

● **Another solution is to** update to more robust antivirus software.
もう１つの解決策はより頑強なウイルス対策ソフトに更新することです。

● **Probably one of the best things to do is to** use multi-factor authentication, namely using two or more different factors to achieve authentication.　恐らく、**最良の方法の１つ**は多要素認証、つまり複数の異なる要素の組み合わせを用いて認証を行う方式を使用することです。

Give It a Try! Mini-Presentation

Based on the Model, give a presentation using the Presentation Template below.

Model　Japan's Declining Birthrate　🎧 16

The falling birthrate **poses serious problems to** Japan's society **because it will lead to** various economic and social problems such as labor shortage. **Given its potentially negative impact on** the future of Japan, **I would like to suggest the following solutions**.

First and foremost, companies **should** help to create a working environment compatible with a parent's lifestyle. **To this end, I would suggest that** companies offer both maternity and paternity leave to help working parents with childbirth and childcare. This leave should also be longer than it is currently.

Additionally, I feel it would be positive to create nursery and childcare facilities either within the workplace, or conveniently located nearby. This would allow parents to pick up their children easily after work. **Another solution is to** introduce flexible working schedules for parents, **so that** they **can** devote time to looking after their young children at important times of the day.

Certainly, many would argue that marriage and childbirth are a matter of personal choice. **However,** both public and private organizations **should** show more awareness about the future of their workforce and the declining birthrate. As it becomes a more serious social problem that requires urgent attention, the government **should** have a strong political will **to turn the situation around.**

Presentation Template

_____ [*your topic*] poses serious problems to _____

because it will lead to _____ .

Given its negative impacts on _____ ,

I would like to suggest the following solutions.

First and foremost, _____ should _____ .

(To this end, I would suggest that _____ .)

Additionally, I feel it would be positive to _____ .

Another solution is to _____

_____ .

Certainly, many would argue that _____.

However, _____ should _____

to turn the situation around.

参考 **Self-Editing Checklist**

draft（原稿）を書き終わったら persuasive-style presentation（説得型プレゼンテーション）の原稿全体を以下の checklist に照らし合わせて点検し、推敲しましょう。

Content（内容）

☐ Is the content interesting enough to arouse the audience interests?

☐ Is the argument well-focused and well-reasoned?

☐ If sources for facts are used, are they introduced and properly cited (e.g., using the expression, "According to ...,")?

Structure（構成）

☐ Does the introduction section clearly set up the theme of the presentation?

☐ Does the thesis statement clearly establish the purpose and scope of the presentation?

☐ Are the body paragraphs clearly focused on the topic or the thesis statement described in the introduction?

☐ Are the main ideas effectively supported by reasoning, examples, and/or evidence?

☐ Does the presenter use conjunctions and transitional phrases effectively?

☐ Does the conclusion summarize the main arguments?

☐ Does the conclusion effectively remind the intended audience of the message conveyed?

Editing（編集）

☐ Does the draft meet the requirements, assigned by the teacher as outlined in the grading guidelines (e.g., word limit, or presentation time, etc.)?

☐ Does the presenter run spellcheck, and redress grammatical or word errors after writing the first draft?

Check (☑) what you have learned:

☐	the features of two types of a persuasive-style presentation
☐	the structure of two types of a persuasive-style presentation
☐	how to organize and develop a standpoint

Compare & Contrast Type Presentation （比較対照型プレゼンテーション）

2つの事象をいくつかの観点から比較・対照し、その共通点・相違点や長所・短所を明示するプレゼンテーションです。比較の仕方には point-by-point 形式と block 形式があります。point を比較する観点、subject を比較する対象として、例えば Office Work vs. Remote Work を以下のように比較できます。

Point-by-point Type Compare and Contrast Presentation

比較する観点 (point) を軸に2つの対象 (subject) を比較しながら議論を展開します。

	Subject 1 (Office Work)	Subject 2 (Remote Work)
Point 1: Time Management	9-5 workday highly controlled at the office	Flexible: work from anywhere, anytime
Point 2: Interaction with colleagues	Face-to-face meetings many opportunities for interaction	Online meetings few opportunities for interaction ⇒ isolation & loneliness

Block Type Compare and Contrast Presentation

対象 (subject) ごとに2つの観点 (point) から議論を展開し、全体的に比較します。

	Point 1 (Time Management)	Point 2 (Interaction with Colleagues)
Subject 1: Office Work	9-5 workday highly controlled at the office	Face-to-face meetings many opportunities for interaction
Subject 2: Remote Work	Flexible: work from anywhere, anytime	Online meetings few opportunities for interaction ⇒ isolation & loneliness

Write a Draft of Your Presentation!

Unit 1~3 で学習したことに基づき、最終プレゼンテーションに向けて、あなた自身のプレゼンテーションの原稿を、次の段階（Step 1~ Step 8）の順に作成しましょう。

Work on your presentation draft, based on what you have learned in Unit 1, 2, and 3. Follow the Steps (from Step 1 to Step 8).

Step 1 Choose a Topic

プレゼンテーション原稿を作成するうえで、最初に直面する難しい作業がトピック選択です。次のような条件を考慮して選択しましょう。

Choose the topic of your presentation, by taking into consideration the following checklist.

Checklist of Topic Selection

☐	時間：与えられた時間 **e.g.** プレゼンテーションの時間は 5 ～ 20 分か 20 分以上か？
☐	得意分野：プレゼンターが知識や経験を持っているトピックか？
☐	興味：プレゼンターがリサーチをして楽しい、興味のあるトピックか？
☐	専門性：プレゼンターが扱えない程、複雑でないか？　専門的過ぎないか？
☐	範囲、具体性：広範過ぎる話題の場合、もっと絞り込みができないか？ **e.g.** ×宇宙開発→△火星における生物→○火星に生命体は存在するか？
☐	独創性：オーディエンスにとって新しい情報や内容が含まれているか？ あるいは、よくあるトピックでも切り口が斬新か？

Task

Which topics are appropriate for a presentation you give to your classmates? If not appropriate, how would you change them?

1. About baseball　　　　　　　　　　　　（　　　　　　　　　　　　）
2. Useful apps for learning English for university students

　　　　　　　　　　　　　　　　　　　（　　　　　　　　　　　　）
3. Top 10 world's most popular travel destinations　（　　　　　　　　　　）
4. COVID-19　　　　　　　　　　　　（　　　　　　　　　　　　）
5. The pros and cons of introducing speaking tests in entrance examinations

　　　　　　　　　　　　　　　　　　　（　　　　　　　　　　　　）

Step 2 Brainstorm Your Ideas on Topic

プレゼンテーションのテーマ・トピックを考えるとき、思いついたことを紙に書き出します。適切か不適切かなどの評価や判断を下さずに、浮かんだアイディアをためらわずに箇条書きにしま

36

す。最初は字下げ（indent）にこだわらずに、また英語、日本語が混じっても構いません。日本語を使った場合、後で英訳しましょう。

1. Brainstorming: Get your ideas down on paper.

例：自己紹介

Main Thematic Topic: Self-introduction

my personal history from birth through high school days

where I was born   where I was brought up

my university life   my study / major   the subjects I am interested in

my extracurricular activities / club (high school) / club (university)

my part-time job / tutor   my hobbies / interests

listening to music   my favorite music / artists / songs

---

2. List your ideas in the structure.

上記の情報に関してアイディアの重要度を考え、提示順やアイディアのグループ化・階層化を考えて structure にまとめます。階層化には字下げ（indent）が有効です。Topic, Subtopic のようなグループ名や 1, 2 のような番号をつけると原稿の作成に便利です。

First, categorize information with appropriate headings. Think about which are main topics and which are subtopics.

Main Thematic Topic: Self-introduction
I. Main Topic 1: My Personal History
    Subtopic: From Birth through High School Days
      1. Where I was born
      2. Where I was brought up
II. Main Topic 2: My University Life
    Subtopic: My Study
      1. My major
      2. The subjects I am interested in
    Subtopic: My Extracurricular Activities
      1. Club (high school)
      2. Club (university)
    Subtopic: My Part-time Job
     Tutor
III. Main Topic 3: My Hobbies
    Subtopic: Listening to Music
     My favorite music
     My favorite artists / songs

---

structure を作成した後で、プレゼンテーションの時間を考えて、情報を削除したり、もっと強調

すべきところは加筆したりすることも重要です。

Step 3　Flow Chart

フローチャートであなたのプレゼンテーションスタイル、タイプを選びましょう。
スタイルは Unit 2, 3 で扱ったものを中心とします。

Decide the style of your presentation, using the flow chart below.

$\boxed{\text{主張したい意見がある}}$
　　　→ **Yes** の場合：⇒ **persuasive-style presentation**
　　　　　　　　$\boxed{\text{解決させたい問題（issue）がある}}$
　　　　　　　　　　→ **Yes** の場合：問題に対して解決策を提案したい
　　　　　　　　　　　　　⇒ **problem-solving type presentation** (=proposal type)
　　　　　　　　　　→ **No** の場合：現状などに対して原因などを分析したい
　　　　　　　　　　　　　⇒ **opinion-building type presentation** (=analysis type)
　　　→ **No** の場合：⇒ **informative-style presentation**
　　　　　　　　$\boxed{\text{情報の提示順に優先順位がある}}$
　　　　　　　　　　→ **Yes** の場合：手続き的、時系列的順序がある
　　　　　　　　　　　　　⇒ **procedural-type presentation / time-order type presentation**
　　　　　　　　　　→ **No** の場合：どの情報も同じくらい重要である
　　　　　　　　　　　　　⇒ **listing-type presentation**

Step 4　Organize Your Presentation into Structure (Outline)

トピックやスタイル・タイプが決定したら、いきなり本文から書き出すのではなく、情報を階層化した structure (outline) を作成しましょう。[Unit 1, 2, 3 参照]

Summarize your main ideas and supporting details into an outline structure.

Title:
Introduction:
　　　　　Background of the Topic
　　　　　Thesis Statement
Body:
　　　Main Idea 1
　　　　　　Supporting Details
　　　Main Idea 2
　　　　　　Supporting Details
　　　Main Idea 3
　　　　　　Supporting Details
Conclusion:

Step 5   Write the First Draft of Your Presentation

まず、アウトラインの Thesis Statement や Main Idea から原稿（draft）を書き出しましょう。Supporting Details には Main Idea に関する理由・例・証拠となるデータなど詳しい情報を付け加えていきます。Supporting Details をどのくらい長くするか、詳しくするかはプレゼンターの知識・情報量や与えられたプレゼンテーションの時間にもよります。

Based on the structure, write sentences centering on the key words and phrases you used in the structure. For supporting details, add reasons, examples, and/or evidence.

Step 6   Edit Your First Draft

Unit 2, 3 の Self-Editing Checklist を基に、first draft を推敲しましょう。

Based on the Self-Editing Checklist, edit your first draft.

Step 7   Peer Review

first draft をクラスメートに読んでもらって、レビューし合いましょう。

Have your classmates read and review the first draft with each other.

Presenter's Name: _____

Peer Feedback					
Topic トピックの面白さ / 適切さ	☹	☹	😐	🙂	🙂
Content 内容の適切さ	☹	☹	😐	🙂	🙂
Structure 原稿の構成	☹	☹	😐	🙂	🙂
Transition アイディアを繋ぐ表現	☹	☹	😐	🙂	🙂

Reviewer's Comments: _____
_____

Step 8   Write the Second Draft of Your Presentation

クラスメートの review や comments も考慮して、second draft に取り組みます。

Work on your second draft, taking into consideration your partner's review and comments.

Unit 4 Making Effective Slides

You will learn:

1. effective fonts and font sizes
2. effective use of color and images
3. how to use animation effectively (option)

Warm-up

Read the textual information, then discuss in pairs which slide, either Slide 1 or Slide 2, is more effective. Write down what you notice in the memo.

Textual information

Today, I'd like to tell you about my favorite place. I love walking around Osaka Castle. What's the best time of year to visit? In Spring, you can enjoy seeing cherry blossoms. In Autumn, you can enjoy seeing red and yellow leaves. All year round, you can enjoy delicious food such as *Takoyaki* and *Okonomiyaki*.

Slide 1: Bullet Chart

What's the best time of year to visit?

- Spring: **Cherry blossoms**.

- Autumn: **Red and yellow leaves**.

- All year round: **Delicious foods** (e.g., *Takoyaki, Okonomiyaki*).

Slide 2: With Pictures

What's the best time of year to visit?

Memo: _____

_____

_____

40

Key Point 1　　Effective Fonts and Font Sizes

1. 欧文フォントは「セリフ体」と「サンセリフ体」に大別されます。セリフ体は、Times New Roman や Century など、縦線に比べて横線が細く、文字の端に飾り (serif) がついているフォントです。一方、サンセリフ体は、線の太さが一定で、飾りがついていない (sans serif = without serif) フォントです。視認性が高いため、スライドには、Arial、Segoe UI、Calibri、Helvetica などのサンセリフ体がおすすめです。

2. 書体の種類は全体的に **2 種類まで**がすっきりした印象になります。

3. 1 枚のスライドに入れる文字は、多くても **6 行で 1 行 6 語**程度までにとどめましょう。

4. 文字の大きさは、タイトルは **36 ポイント以上**、本文は **24 ポイント以上**ぐらいがいいでしょう。

5. 文字数が多いときは、文章の要点を抽出した「**箇条書き**」 **bullet chart** を使います。

セリフ体の例	サンセリフ体の例
Times New Roman at 66 pt.	Helvetica at 66 pt.
Century at 54 pt.	Arial at 54 pt.
Baskerville at 48 pt.	**Franklin Gothic at 48 pt.**

Task 1　　Look at the following slides and compare the designs. Compare the font and the size of the texts in particular.

1.

History of Osaka Castle: Quiz

1. When was Osaka Castle built?　　　1. In 1585

2. Who built it?　　　2. Toyotomi Hideyoshi

3. How many times was it burned down?　　　3. Twice

2.

History of Osaka Castle: Quiz

1. **When** was Osaka Castle built?　　　1. In 1585

2. **Who** built it?　　　2. Toyotomi Hideyoshi

3. **How many times** was it burned down?　　　3. Twice

Memo:

_____

_____

Task 2 Look at the following slides and compare the designs. Compare the length of the texts in particular.

1. Text Slide

> **History of Osaka Castle**
>
> • Osaka Castle was built in 1585 by Toyotomi Hideyoshi who aimed to unify Japan.
> • It took two years to build the castle, but it was burned and destroyed in the Osaka Summer War in1615.
> • It was rebuilt during the Tokugawa period but was destroyed by fire again in 1665 when lightning struck it. From then, Osaka Castle remained without a keep.
> • The current castle was built in 1931 with donations from the citizens of the city.

2. Bullet Chart

> **History of Osaka Castle**
>
> • In 1585: Built by Toyotomi Hideyoshi.
>
> • In1615: Burned and destroyed (in the Osaka Summer War).
>
> • In 1665: Destroyed by fire again.
>
> • In 1931: Rebuilt with donations.

Memo: _____

_____

Key Point 2 Effective Use of Color and Images

1. PowerPoint では、文字を目立たせたいときは、背景が白の場合は、濃い色、青などが見やすいです。赤や黄色はチカチカして、読みにくいです。プレゼンテーションを行う教室が暗い場合は、スライドの背景を紺色などの暗い色にし、文字を白抜きや黄色っぽい明るい色にするとコントラストがはっきりして、見やすくなります。

2. PowerPoint では、コンテンツに関連のあるビジュアル・イメージを上手く使いビジュアル化していきます。

Task 3 Look at the following slides and compare the designs. Which slide is more effective?

1.

> **What's the best time of year to visit?**
>
> • Spring: **Cherry blossoms.**
>
> • Autumn: **Red and yellow leaves.**
>
> • All year round: **Delicious foods**
>
>   (e.g., *Takoyaki, Okonomiyaki*).

2.

> **What's the best time of year to visit?**
>
> • Spring: Cherry blossoms.
>
> • Autumn: Red and yellow leaves.
>
> • All year round: Delicious foods
>
>   (e.g., *Takoyaki, Okonomiyaki*).

Memo: _____

_____

Task 4 Look at the following slides and compare the designs. Which slide is more effective?

1.

2.

Memo:

Key Point 3　How to Use Animation Effectively (Option)

PowerPoint では、「アニメーション」を設定して、スライド内の文字、画像、図表などに動く演出を加えることができます。例えば、箇条書きの項目を一つずつ順に表示したり、クイズで答えの部分を後から出したりしたいときには、「フェード」や「ワイプ」を使います。「アニメーションウィンドウ」を開いて、表示するタイミングや速度を調整できます。ただし、使いすぎは逆効果で、オーディエンスの気を散らすことさえあります。

PowerPoint では、「画面切り替え」を設定して、スライドを切り替える際の動きの演出をすることができます。様々な動きを選ぶだけで簡単に設定でき、切り替えの速さも「時間」で調整できます。ただし、アニメーションと同様に、使い過ぎは逆効果になります。

Key Expressions

🎧 17

■ Expressions for Introducing the Contents Slide

● **My presentation has** four parts.
お話する内容は4つあります。

● **Next, I would like to show you** my favorite place.
次に、私のお気に入りの場所をお見せしたいと思います。

● **Please take a look at this slide**.
こちらのスライドをご覧ください。

● **Here you can see** Taikobashi in Sumiyoshi Taisha.
こちらに住吉大社の太鼓橋が見えます。

● **Please look at** Taikobashi in Sumiyoshi Taisha.
住吉大社の太鼓橋を見てください。

● **If you look carefully here, you will see** a small tree.
注意深く見ると、小さい木が見えます。

Give It a Try!   Mini-Presentation

Based on the Model, give a presentation, using the Presentation Template below.

このユニットで学んだことを活用し、「**My Favorite Place**」で作成した自分のスクリプトに8枚のスライドをつけ、**PowerPoint** のスライドを作成してみましょう。

スライドは基本的に次の項目で構成されています。Title slide, Table of Contents slide, Body slides, Conclusion slide, Appreciation slide, Reference slide などです。

Model My Favorite Place: Osaka

My Favorite Place: Osaka

YAMADA Hanako
123456789
Faculty of Tourism
Academic Presentation University
July 7, 2024

1

Contents

• My favorite place: Osaka

• History of Osaka castle

• Things you can do in Osaka

• What's the best time of year to visit?

2

Taikobashi in Sumiyoshi Taisha

Sumiyoshi Taisha was established in 211.

Look at the reflection! You know why it's called Taikobashi or "drum bridge".

In Shinto mythology, Izanagi is the "father" of Sumiyoshi Taisha's patron deities.

Images taken from Saigen Jiro(CC0 1.0)Public Domain Dedication

3

History of Osaka Castle: Quiz

1. **When** was Osaka Castle built?

2. **Who** built it?

3. **How many times** was it burned down?

   1. In 1585

   2. Toyotomi Hideyoshi

   3. Twice

4

Things you can do in Osaka

Osaka Museum of History

©Yanajin33 (CC BY-SA 3.0)   ©iStockphoto.com/Promo_Link

5

Things you can do around the castle

• Spring: **cherry blossoms**.
• Autumn: **red and yellow leaves**.
• All year round: **delicious foods** (e.g., *Takoyaki*).

6

Thank you for your attention.

If you have any questions, please contact me:
hanakoyamada@zmail.ac.jp

7

References

Ohtani, K. (1994). *Osaka gaku* [Osaka studies]. Keiei-shoin.

Sumiyoshi Taisha. (n.d.). Overview and history. Retrieved November 25, 2022, from https://www.sumiyoshitaisha.net/

The Official Osaka Travel Guide. (n.d.). About Osaka. Retrieved November 25, 2022, from https://osaka-info.jp/spot/osaka-castle-main-keep/

8

Model Script My Favorite Place: Osaka   18

Hello everyone. I am Hanako Yamada. **Today, I'd like to talk about my favorite place. My presentation has** four **parts. First, I will explain** why I like Osaka. **Next, I will talk about** the history of Osaka Castle by giving a quiz. **Then, I will describe** things you can do in Osaka. **Finally, I will talk about** when the best time of the year to visit is.

Let me start by telling you briefly about why I like Osaka. I was born in Osaka and grew up near Sumiyoshi Taisha. Sumiyoshi Taisha is one of the oldest shrines in Japan. It was established in 211. Do you know Taikobashi in Sumiyoshi Taisha? Please take a look at this slide. If you look carefully here, you can see the reflection! Now, you know why it's called Taikobashi, drum bridge. I remember visiting there for Shichi-go-san with my family. Taikobashi was very steep, so I remember feeling scared to cross the bridge. My childhood memories of the bridge remain with me today, and still give me a feeling of pleasure every time I see the bridge.

Since I grew up in Osaka, I would often enjoy visiting Osaka Castle with my family and friends. For this, I would like to give you a quiz about Osaka Castle. Do you know when it was built? The answer is it was built in 1585. Do you know who built it? That's right, Toyotomi Hideyoshi. Here is the last question. Do you know how many times it was burned down? Yes, that's correct: Twice. So, the current castle was built with donations from the citizens of the city.

In Osaka, **you can do many things. You can** visit the Osaka Museum of History, eat delicious food, and enjoy live concerts.

So, when is the best time to visit? In spring, you can enjoy cherry blooms around the castle and in autumn, you can see beautiful red and yellow leaves. Most importantly, all year round, you can enjoy delicious foods. You certainly won't be disappointed!

Today I introduced my favorite places in Osaka. **Here is the list of references. Thank you for listening. Do you have any questions?**

Presentation Template

Hello everyone. I am _____. Today, I'd like to talk about my favorite place.

My presentation has _____ parts. First, I will explain _____.

Next, I will talk about _____. Then, I will describe _____.

Finally, I will talk about _____.

Let me start by telling you briefly about _____. _____

_____.

In _____ , you can do many things. You can _____ .

_____ . _____ .

Today I introduced my favorite _____ . Here is the list of references.

Thank you for listening. Do you have any questions?

❗ Tips for describing your favorite city

お気に入りの場所についてプレゼンテーションする際は、客観的な事実のみならず、なぜ好きなのか、どのようなところが好きなのか、などについて主観も入れて話すと魅力的なプレゼンテーションになります。ガイドブックには載っていないような自分のお勧めを語ってみるのもよいでしょう。下記の例を参考にしてください。

My favorite place is _____ .

> *My favorite place is* a café near my house. Every Saturday, I go there to relax and enjoy reading some fashion magazines.

I like to visit _____ .

> *I like to visit* a café near my house. I usually go there after the gym on weekends.

I enjoy visiting _____ .

> *I enjoy visiting* Osaka Castle in autumn as I can see beautiful red and yellow leaves. Walking around the castle is so refreshing.

You should definitely try/buy/see _____ .

> *You should definitely try* the Japanese tea ceremony. I love green tea. It's thick, delicious, and very healthy.

You can enjoy _____ .

> Osaka Castle is my favorite place. In spring, *you can enjoy* seeing cherry blossoms. It's in the city, but you can still enjoy nature there.

Check (☑) what you have learned:

☐	how to use effective fonts and font sizes for slides
☐	how to use color and images effectively
☐	how to use animation effectively for slides (option)

Unit 5 Visualizing Textual Information

You will learn:

1. why you should visualize textual information
2. how to make appropriate diagrams
3. how to explain textual information in an effective way

Warm-up

In pairs, compare the text information with the two slides below. Discuss the advantages and disadvantages of each.

Textual information

Today, I'd like to tell you about the microplastic pollution cycle. People waste a lot of plastic every year. Used plastic is washed away by rain and carried to the ocean, and eventually becomes fine particles, namely, microplastics. In the ocean, fish eat them. Then people eat the fish and ingest the microplastic.

Slide 1: Bullet Chart

Microplastic Pollution Cycle

· People waste plastic
· Used plastic becomes microplastic
· Fish eat them
· People eat the fish

Slide 2: Diagram

Microplastic Pollution Cycle

Plastic

People

Microplastic

Fish

Memo: _____

_____

_____

Key Point 1　Types of Diagrams

PowerPoint には、効率よく図解を作成するための「SmartArt グラフィックス」が備わっています。SmartArt を使うときには、次の A ～ G の図形のひな型から適切なものを選んで利用します。

	要素間の関係	図形の種類	図形のイメージ
変化	時の流れ、順序、因果 例）原料が製品になるまでのプロセス	⇒ A［手順］	
	循環、繰り返し 例）使用済みペットボトルを原料として再び同製品を作るプロセス	⇒ B［循環］	
構造	階層、組織図 例）地域自主防災の組織構造	⇒ C ［階層構造］	
	階層、上下 例）低所得者層、中間層、富裕層からなる所得別人口構成	⇒ D ［ピラミッド］	
	包含、共通点 例）電車だけバスだけ電車とバスの両方という通学時の利用状況	⇒ E［集合］	
並列	表、グループ化 例）ワールドカップサッカー出場国のグループごとの組み合わせ	⇒ F［リスト］	
	全体と各部分、要素比較 例）緊急度と重要度の組み合わせによる仕事の優先順位	⇒ G ［マトリクス］	

Key Point 2　Making Diagrams

文章を図解するときには、次のような手順で行います。

1. 文章のキーワードを抜き出して、箇条書きにする
   ↓
2. 各要素をグループに分け、その間の関係を考える
   ↓
3. その関係を表すのに最適な図形を選んで、図解する

要素間の関係を見つけてそれを図解するという作業では、まず、その関係が「SmartArt グラフィックス」の [変化]、[構造]、[並列] のうちの「どのパターンに当てはまるか」を考えます。そして、PowerPoint の [挿入] タブから [SmartArt] ボタンへと進み、適切な図解を選びます。

Task 1
For the following textual information and Bullet Chart, choose from A-G above which diagram to use. Then make its diagram.

1. 3 つのタイプの SNS

SNS は、どのメディアを主に使うかに応じて、次の 3 つのタイプに分けられます。文章は LINE, X（Twitter）、写真は Instagram, Pinterest, Snapchat、動画は YouTube, TikTok, niconico が有名です。

Bullet Chart

Main Uses of Social Media

- Text: LINE, X (Twitter)
- Photo: Instagram, Pinterest, Snapchat
- Video: YouTube, TikTok, niconico

Diagram (F) (Example)

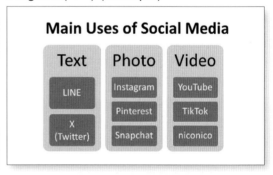

2. 学生の部屋選び

家賃の高低と学校へのアクセスの善し悪しによって 4 つの要素に分類しました。ほとんどの学生が家賃が安く学校に近い部屋を選びたいと言っています。

Bullet Chart

How do Students Choose Their Apartment?
✓ Four factors:
　high or low rent and good or bad access
　to school
✓ Their choice:
　a room with a low rent and close to school

Diagram (　　)

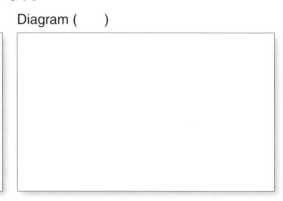

3. 昆虫食

昆虫食のメリットの1つは、加工がしやすいことです。まず昆虫を乾燥して、次にそれをパウダーにします。すると、そのパウダーはパン、クッキー、せんべい、パスタなどのさまざまな食品に容易に加工できます。

Bullet Chart   Diagram (   )

Insect Food: Easy to Process

· Dry the insects
· Grind them into a powder.
· Process the powder into various foods
  (bread, cookies, crackers, pasta)

---

4. カーボンニュートラル

植物はバイオ燃料の原料になります。バイオ燃料は燃やすと CO_2 を排出しますが、植物は CO_2 を吸収して成長します。すなわち、排出される CO_2 と吸収される CO_2 は同じです。

Bullet Chart   Diagram (   )

Carbon Neutrality

· Plants are made into biofuels.
· Biofuels emit CO_2 when burned.
· Plants absorb CO_2 and grow.

CO_2 emitted = CO_2 absorbed

Key Expressions

🎧 19

- This diagram **shows** the microplastic pollution cycle.
  この図は、マイクロプラスチックの汚染サイクル**を表しています**。

- The used plastic eventually becomes fine particles, **namely**, microplastics.
  使用済みのプラスチックはやがて細かい粒子、**すなわち**マイクロプラスチックになります。

- Social Media **can be divided into** three types, **depending on** the medium used.
  SNS は、使用するメディア**に応じて**、3つのタイプ**に分けられます**。

- **This is a list of** social media divided by main uses.
  これは主な用途別に分けた SNS の**一覧です**。

- Words **fall into** four types.
  単語は4つのタイプ**に分類されます**。

- The words appear **in a wide range of genres** and **have a high frequency**.

  これらの単語は**幅広いジャンル**に登場し、**頻度が高い**です。

- Thus, the first words we must memorize are type A, **followed by** type B.

  したがって、最初に覚えるべき単語はタイプ A で、**その後に**タイプ B が続きます。

- **What do you think of** this matrix diagram?

  このマトリクス図を**どう思いますか**。

- **As indicated by this diagram,** most students want to choose a room with low rent and close to school.

  この図で**示されているように**、ほとんどの学生が家賃が安く、学校に近い部屋を選びたいと考えています。

- **On the whole, we can conclude that** organisms remain balanced despite fluctuations in their overall numbers.

  全体として、生物は全体の数が変動しても釣り合いが保たれている**と結論づける**ことができます。

Give It a Try! Mini-Presentation

Based on the Model, make a bullet chart, make the diagram, and give a presentation using the Presentation Template below.

Model Words We Must Memorize   20

> **This diagram represents** what types of words we must memorize in language learning. Words fall into four types. **Let me explain each.**
>
> **The upper left part** (A) **shows** high-frequency words in a wide range of fields. **The lower left part** (B) **includes** low-frequency words in a wide range of fields. **The upper right** (C) **displays** high-frequency words in a narrow range of fields. **The lower right** (D) **features** low-frequency words in a narrow range of fields. **On the whole, we can conclude that** the first words we must memorize are type A, followed by type B, and then type C. Type D can be looked up in the dictionary.

1. Bullet Chart

Words We Must Memorize

2. Diagram   appropriate diagram (   )

Words We Must Memorize

Presentation Template

This diagram represents _____. Let me explain each. The upper left part shows _____, the lower left part includes _____, the upper right part displays _____, and the lower right part features _____. On the whole, we can conclude that _____.

Check (☑) what you have learned:

☐	the characteristics of diagrams
☐	how to make appropriate diagrams for textual information
☐	how to explain diagrams

Unit 6 Visualizing Quantitative Data

You will learn:

1. what kind of chart to use based on data types
2. how to design charts
3. how to explain quantitative data in an effective way

Warm-up

Read the textual information, then discuss in pairs which slide, either Slide 1 or Slide 2, is more visually effective. Write down what you notice in the memo.

Textual Information

Today, I'm going to talk about the average temperature for four seasons in three regions – Hokkaido, Tokyo, and Okinawa. As can be seen, overall the temperatures are the lowest in January and the highest in July across the three regions. For example, the January temperature in Tokyo is 5.5 degrees and the July one is 25.7 degrees. On the other hand, one noteworthy point is that only Hokkaido records freezing temperatures, which is 3.2 degrees below zero.

Slide 1: Table

Average temperature of three regions (°C)

	Jan.	Apr.	Jul.	Oct.
Hokkaido	-3.2	7.3	21.1	12.1
Tokyo	5.5	14.3	25.7	18.0
Okinawa	17.3	21.5	29.1	25.5

Slide 2: Chart

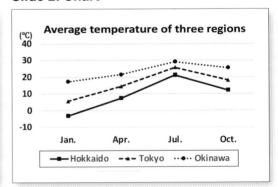

Memo:

54

Key Point 1   Types of Charts and Appropriate Data

グラフを用いることで、データ全体の傾向や特徴がわかりやすくなります。見栄えだけでグラフを選ぶとかえってわかりにくくなることがありますので、データの種類や特徴に合ったグラフを選ぶようにしましょう。

....

Task 1   Read the description of each chart and fill in the space with the appropriate chart name from the box.

Bar Chart	Line Chart	Pie Chart
Radar Chart	XY (Scatter) Chart	

1.（　　　　　　　　　　）
棒グラフは棒の長さで<u>数量の大小を比較</u>するのに適しています。大きい順に左から並べることもあります。
例）学年別による各高校の１週間における図書室利用者数

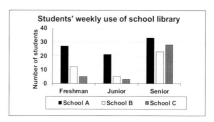

2.（　　　　　　　　　　）
円グラフは円全体を 100% として<u>各項目の割合</u>を表すのに適しています。通常、右回りに大きい順に並べ、最後を「その他（Other）」にします。ただし、「賛成」「どちらかといえば賛成」のような同じ傾向の項目を順に並べて書く方がわかりやすい場合、数の大きい順に並べない方がよいこともあります。
例）Ａ組の好きなスポーツの割合

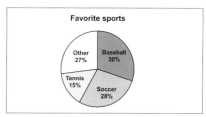

3.（　　　　　　　　　　）
折れ線グラフは時間の変化による<u>数量の変化</u>を表すのに適しています。縦軸の目盛りは０から始めますが、変化がわかりづらい場合、横軸に波線を入れて途中を省略したり、グラフ右の縦軸に別の目盛りを設定したりすることもあります。
例）３社の過去４か月の売り上げ

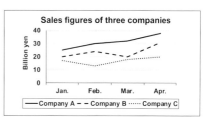

4.（　　　　　　　　　　）
散布図は<u>２つのデータに関係があるかどうか</u>を表すのに適しています。しかし、関係があるからといって、因果関係があるとは言えません。
例）Ｂ組の生徒の身長と体重の関係

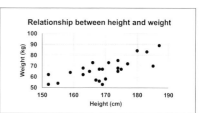

5.（　　　　　　　　　　）
レーダーグラフは<u>全体に対する複数個の数量の比較</u>を１つのグラフで表すのに適しています。数値は大きくなればなるほどよいため、小さければよいものについては、数値の単位を逆転させます。また、単位の異なるデータを用いる場合は比率等に変換します。
例）生徒Ａの５教科の点数とクラス平均点との比較

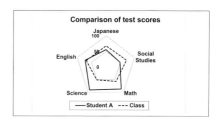

Key Point 2　Chart Design

PowerPoint でのグラフ作成は、以下の手順を取ります。

1. 左図のように、[挿入] タブ内にある [グラフ] をクリック。

2. 中図のように、「グラフの挿入」ウィンドウが表示されるので、データの種類に応じて使用するグラフを選択。

3. 右図のように、スプレッドシートに数値やカテゴリー / 系列名などを入力。

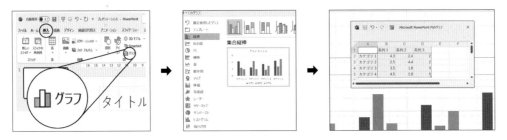

....

Task 2　Choose three tables from (1) – (5) below and design the charts. Remember the chart characteristics explained in Key Point 1 when designing.

(1) Average per-game attendance of baseball by team　　　　　　　　　(Thousand)

	2001	2006	2011	2016
Team A	30	31	35	28
Team B	24	22	18	23
Team C	34	33	30	31

(2) Annual average costs of eating out for three types of cuisine by city　　　(Yen)

	Japanese meals	Western meals	Chinese meals
City A	24,145	13,471	5,320
City B	22,807	8,053	4,428
City C	21,846	14,762	2,773

(3) Average test scores of the whole class and Student A's test scores

	Japanese	Social Studies	English
Class average	60	65	71
Student A	88	84	58

(4) Types of TV program university students watch　　　　　　　　　　　(%)

Entertainment	Sports	Informative	News	Other
47	19	15	12	7

(5) Highest temperature and Store A's cold drink sales during summer

	Jun.1	Jun.16	Jul.1	Jul.16	Aug.1	Aug.16	Sep.1	Sep.16
Temp. (℃)	16	21	26	35	38	36	31	28
Sales (¥)	23,000	29,000	36,000	48,000	56,000	50,000	38,000	35,000

Key Point 3   A Listener-friendly Explanation about Data

グラフ中のデータを説明する場合は、数値等を単に列挙するのではなく、(1) グラフ全体の特徴、(2) その特徴を顕著に表す例、そして、あれば (3) 例外や特記すべき例、の順番に述べます。

Task 3   Compare Text A and Text B and discuss with your partner which explanation is more appropriate to describe the characteristics of the chart.

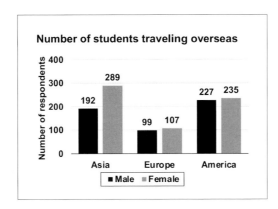

Text A   The bar chart shows the number of male and female students traveling abroad by region. First, 192 male students took a trip to Asia and 289 female students went to these areas. Second, 99 boys traveled to European countries while 107 girls toured to these countries. Third, 227 male students traveled to American regions and 235 female students took a trip to these areas.

Text B   The bar chart shows the number of male and female students traveling abroad by region. Overall, more female students went abroad than male students. For example, a slightly higher number of girls traveled to Europe and America than boys, and the difference is eight, respectively. However, a large difference was found in Asia. That is, 192 boys and 289 girls went to the areas.

▥ Expressions for the Chart in General

● **This chart demonstrates** the average temperatures for four seasons in three regions.

このグラフは、3地域における4つの季節の平均気温を示しています。

● **It is clear that** the difference of the average temperature across the three regions becomes large in January but small in July.

3地域の平均気温の差は、1月に大きく7月に小さくなっていることがわかります。

● **These results indicate that** Student A is good at science-related subjects and weak at humanity-related ones.

これらの結果から、生徒Aは理系科目が得意で文系科目が苦手であることがわかります。

▥ Expressions for the Chart Trends

● The number of library users is higher in the order of School A, School B, and School C. **Meanwhile**, the order is different for the seniors.

図書館利用者数はA校、B校、C校の順で多くなっています。一方で、3年生については順番が異なっています。

● Baseball and soccer **accounted for almost two thirds of** the entire preference.

野球とサッカーは好み全体の**3分の2近く**を占めていました。

● There was **a gradual increase in** sales by Company A from January to April.

1月から4月にかけて、A社の売り上げが**緩やかに増加**していました。

● Sales of Company C **remained almost unchanged** for the four month period.

C社の売り上げは、4か月間**ほとんど横ばい**でした。

● **The taller** students become, **the heavier** they become.

生徒の身長が**高くなればなるほど、体重が増えます。**

● Student A **scored highest in** Science at nearly 100 whereas the score of Social Studies was the lowest at around 50.

生徒Aは、理科が100点に近い**高得点**だったのに対し、社会は50点前後と最も低い点数でした。

● Compared with the scores in Math and Science, Student A's scores in Japanese and Social Studies **were below the class average**.

数学と理科の点数に比べ、生徒Aの国語と社会の点数は**クラス平均点を下回っていました。**

Give It a Try! Mini-Presentation

Based on the Model, survey your classmates, design a chart, and give a presentation using the Presentation Template below. For the survey, think about one or two questions you would like to investigate.

Model   Mini-survey Results on Study Time

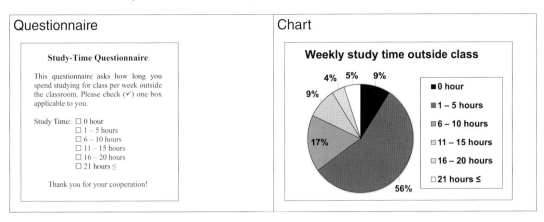

Model Script   Mini-survey Results on Study Time   22

Please look at the pie chart. This chart describes my classmates' weekly study-time outside the classroom. Overall, it is clear that the majority of the students didn't spend a lot of time previewing and reviewing for class. For example, 65% of them previewed and reviewed for class less than six hours. Meanwhile, it is revealed that nearly one tenth of the students, which is 9%, spent more than 15 hours a week for study outside the classroom. These results indicate that my classmates didn't study hard during the week related to the class.

Presentation Template

Please look at the _____ chart. This chart describes _____ . Overall, it is clear that the majority of _____ . For example, _____ . Meanwhile, it is revealed that _____ . These results indicate that _____ .

Check (☑) what you have learned:

☐	appropriate charts to use based on data types
☐	how to design charts
☐	how to explain quantitative data in a listener-friendly way

COLUMN

誤解を与えるグラフ

グラフはデータを効果的に、かつ瞬時に聞き手に伝えることができるという利点があります。しかし、見栄えをよくするためにさまざまな工夫をした結果、かえってデータの伝える事実を歪めてしまうことがあります。ここでは 2 つの例を見てみます。

3D グラフ

図 1 はペットについての人気投票の結果を 3D グラフにしたものです。一見すると、ネコ派の方がイヌ派よりも多く見えます。しかし、この結果を図 2 の通常のグラフにすると、実際はイヌ派とネコ派は同数であることがわかります。

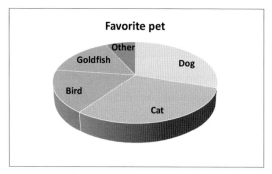

図 1　3D グラフ

図 2　通常のグラフ

絵グラフ

図 3 はメモ取りにパソコンを使用する人数を絵の大きさで表しています。A 組の使用者数は B 組の 3 倍ですが、一見すると差はそれ以上に見えます。図 4 のように、絵の大きさによる差は 9 倍であるため、実際の差より大きく見えてしまっています。

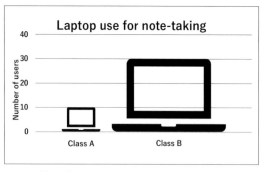

図 3　絵の大きさによる比較

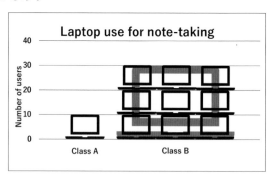

図 4　絵の大きさによる実際の差

このように、効果的と思われる工夫がかえってデータの伝える事実を歪めてしまうことがありますので、そのような工夫が本当に必要かよく考えなければなりません。

60

Mission ❷

Make Slides for Your Presentation!

Unit 4~6 で学習したことに基づき、Mission 1 であなたが作成した原稿を使って、最終プレゼンテーション用のスライドを作成してみましょう。

Step 1　Overall Slide Structure

スライド全体は、基本的には次の5種類のスライドから構成されています。この基本の流れにそって、下の Tips に留意しながら、スライドを作成していきます。

Learn the overall slide structure and tips for making slides.

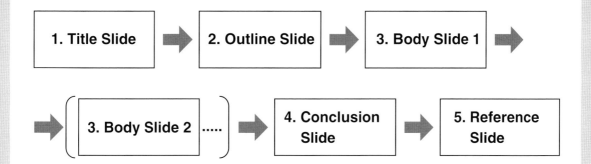

> **! Tips for making slides**
>
> スライドを作成するときには、次の5つのポイントに注意しましょう。大切なのは、オーディエンスが「読む」のではなく「見る」スライドにするということです。
> 1. 「1スライド・1メッセージ」を意識する。
> 2. 「1スライド・30秒前後」で話すのが基本。(すなわち、持ち時間が10分なら、作成するスライド数は約20枚となる。)
> 3. 「1スライド・6行6語」程度にとどめる。
> 4. フォントは視認性が高いサンセリフ体を使い、サイズは「タイトル36pt、本文24pt」以上を心がける。
> 5. 数量データはチャート、文字情報は図解の使用を考える。

Step 2　Make Your Own Slides

Mission 1 で作成した自分の原稿を、PowerPoint を使ってスライドにしていきましょう。

Using PowerPoint, make slides with the following contents.

1. Title Slide

(Example)

Declining Birth Rate in Japan

YAMADA Taro
April 15, 2025

1枚目のスライドには、タイトル、氏名、日付を記入します。必要に応じて、所属、発表会場などを付け加えます。

2. Outline Slide

Outline

1. Actual Conditions
2. Causal Factors
3. Three Solutions

2枚目のスライドは「目次」で、このプレゼンテーションで扱う項目を列挙していきます。Mission 1で作成したOutlineを簡略化して記入しましょう。

3. Body Slide(s)

Actual Conditions

- 2015→2.3
- 2030→1.9
- 2045→1.4

3枚目のスライドから、Bodyのそれぞれの項目を記入していきます。上部にトピックのタイトルをつけ、下部は箇条書きにするのが基本です。必要に応じて、チャートや図解を用いてわかりやすくします。

4. Conclusion Slide

Conclusion

- The declining birthrate
  →collapse of social security
- Provide 10 million yen
  for each newborn baby.

話した内容の簡潔なまとめと締めくくりの言葉を記入します。また、今後の課題 などを示すのもよいでしょう。

5. Reference Slide

References

- Statistics Bureau of Japan. (2025).
  Statistical Handbook
  Retrieved from https://www.stat.go.jp/data/
- The Cabinet Office. (2025).
  Annual Report on the Declining Birthrate.
  Retrieved from https://www8.cao.go.jp/
  whitepaper/

参考にした文献をまとめて記入します。
このスライドの後にもう1枚、謝辞や自分の連絡先を示すスライドを添えることもあります。

Step 3   Check Your Slides

スライドが完成したら、実際に原稿を声に出して読みながら、スライドをチェックしましょう。

In pairs, check each other's slides as you read your drafts aloud and give each other feedback using the chart below.

Presenter's Name: _____

Peer Feedback					
Number of Words 語数の適切さ	☹	☹	😐	🙂	🙂
Fonts フォントの種類・大きさ	☹	☹	😐	🙂	🙂
Images (Photos, Illustrations) 画像	☹	☹	😐	🙂	🙂
Diagrams 図解	☹	☹	😐	🙂	🙂
Charts チャート	☹	☹	😐	🙂	🙂

**Reviewer's
Comments:** _____

_____

_____

_____

Unit 7　Pronunciation Focus

You will learn:

1. effective pronunciation and stress
2. sound changes in phrases and sentences
3. how to read aloud a presentation draft

Warm-up

日本語が高低型言語（Pitch Accent Language）であるのに対して、英語は強弱型言語（Stress Accent Language）と言われます。つまり、単語や文中で、ある部分を強く発音することによって、文全体のバランスを維持しています。より自然で効果的な英語プレゼンテーションを行うために、英語の強勢（stress）を意識しながら発音しましょう。

日本語：高低型	英語：強弱型
テクニック：「テ」を高く読む	tech-**nique** : -nique を**強く**読む
〔高 ↘ 低〕	○ ● 〔●＝強　○＝弱〕

英語を話すときは日本語にない子音、特に [f]、[v]、[r]、[θ]、[ð] などは注意しましょう。母音に関しては、二重母音の [eɪ]、[ou] は「エー」や「オー」のような発音にならないように、また、[au] は house や now のように -ou- や -ow- の綴りで書かれる単語もあるので、[ou] と混同しないよう注意が必要です。リズムについては Pre-Unit を参照してください。

Listen to the following words and sentences paying attention to stress (1-6), pronunciation (7-13), and rhythm (14-15) of each word and sentence. Then, read them aloud in pairs. 23

1. ner-vous　　　2. ex-change　　　3. im-por-tant

4. ad-di-tion-al　　5. op-por-tu-ni-ty　　6. sci-en-ti-fi-cal-ly

7. <u>o</u>nly　　8. all<u>ow</u>　　9. en<u>ough</u>

10. <u>v</u>olunteer　11. br<u>ow</u>n　12. b<u>oth</u>　13. smo<u>oth</u>

14. He was the pioneer of the theory of evolution.

15. The new factory is more environmentally friendly.

Key Point **1**   Intonation and a Pause Unit in Oral Reading   24

〔抑揚〕英文を読むときは、文の種類によってイントネーションが異なります。また、付加疑問文では、語尾の上下により、話し手の多様な感情や態度を表すことができます。

平叙文 （↘）	＊下降調 (descending)：Our school has a "project studies" program.
疑問文 Yes-no question （↗）	＊上昇調 (ascending)：Do you agree with the plan?
疑問文 Wh-question （↘）	＊下降調：What is your opinion about that?
付加疑問文（↗）または（↘）	＊上昇調：Soomi is coming to our party, isn't she?（問いかけ） ＊下降調：Soomi is coming to our party, isn't she?（確認）

Task **1**   In pairs, listen to the following sentences with ascending   25
and descending intonation respectively. Then, read them
aloud in pairs.

1. I'd like to talk about how to prevent bicycle accidents.
2. Do you know how many bicycle accidents happened in your town?
3. How about giving a penalty to those who violate the traffic rules?
4. There are many bicycle accidents in this town, aren't there?

フォワードスラッシュ（/）は、音読では休止単位を、文では意味グループを表します。ダブルスラッシュ（//）は文節グループを表します。例えば、次のAとBの2つの区切り方では、Bの方が意味のまとまりを形成したスラッシュの使い方と言えます。

A. Do you know how / much plastic is / disposed of / in the ocean? //
B. Do you know / how much plastic / is disposed of in the ocean? //

また、スラッシュで区切られたまとまりは英語リズムの単位でもあることから、スラッシュでのまとまりを意識して読むこと（スラッシュ読み）は自然な英語のリズムやイントネーションを身につけることにもつながります。

Task **2**   Following the examples above, put forward and double   26
slashes in each sentence. Then, read them in pairs.

1. I suggest we do some volunteer activities to contribute to our town.
2. For example, we could clean the area around the station once a month.
3. I'm going to report on the part-time jobs done by the students in our school.
4. First of all, I'd like to point out that 30% of the students have part-time jobs.

Key Point 2   Sound Changes in a Phrase and Sentence   27

〔音の変化〕代名詞、助動詞、冠詞、前置詞、接続詞、関係詞などは通常、文中で弱く発音されます。

can [kǽn] → [kⱥn]   I <u>can</u> swim from this side to the other of the river.

that [ðǽt] → [ðⱥt]   This is the subway <u>that</u> goes to my school.

of   [ʌ́v] → [ⱥv]   What kind <u>of</u> color should I wear to the party tonight?

and [ǽnd] → [ⱥn]   Jimmy <u>and</u> Kris have already left for Europe.

....

Task 3   Listen to the following sentences paying attention to the   28
             function words in each sentence. Then, read them in pairs.

1. You can visit me at any time.
2. Let's talk about it over a cup of coffee.
3. Kenji and Yumi watched YouTube instead of studying.
4. Large cars that use a lot of gas are unpopular.
5. The 2025 Osaka Expo can be a great chance to make changes.

〔変化する **t** の発音〕次の語やフレーズでは、[t] の音に注意して発音しましょう。   29

Example 1. 発音が [tn] で終わる語

   例：cer<u>tain</u>, moun<u>tain</u>, wri<u>tten</u> など

Example 2. 発音が [tli] で終わる語

   例：absolu<u>tely</u>, comple<u>tely</u>, defini<u>tely</u>, exac<u>tly</u> など

Example 3. 前の語の発音が [t] で終わり、後ろの語の発音が子音で始まるとき

   例：mus<u>t g</u>o, wri<u>te d</u>own など

....

Task 4   Listen to the following phrases and sentences. Then, take   30
             turns pronouncing them in pairs.

1. the written test   2. absolutely right
3. the best season   4. the most difficult job
5. can't talk   6. must go   7. write down new ideas
8. What he said yesterday was absolutely right.
9. What's the best season for visiting Kyoto?
10. It's the most difficult job we've ever had.
11. I'm sorry I can't talk now. I must go.
12. I always try to write down new ideas in notebooks

Key Point 3   Linking and Consonant Clusters in Phrases and Sentences   31

〔連結〕2つの単語が連続して読まれる場合、最初の語の語末子音と次の語の語頭の母音がつながって、**連結（linking）**という音の変化が起こり、1語のように発音される場合があります。この音変化のルールを知っておくと、発音だけでなく、リスニング力の向上にもつながります。以下の例のように、2語、3語、あるいは文の中で ⌣ の箇所がつながって、1つのかたまりのように聞こえます。

例：What a good idea!   an exam

Task 5   Listen to the audio and read the phrases and sentences in pairs aloud.   32

1. step outside   2. look at
3. There's a big oak tree in front of the bus stop.
4. I'm going to step outside for a breath of fresh air.
5. Some of the students have already gone home.
6. Modern technology makes it so easy to connect with people.
7. Gill looks happier than usual.
8. If you're having trouble with the computer, may I suggest finding someone to help you?
9. They'll be back in an hour.

〔子音連続〕2つの語が連続して、語と語の境界で子音が連続するときの発音です。滑らかに発音できるようにモデル音声を聞いてよく練習しましょう。特に破裂音を含む子音の場合は要注意です。

Example 1. 破裂音 [p]、[t]、[k]、[b]、[d]、[g] が連続するとき   33
　　例：big game   stop by   top down   take care

Example 2. 破裂音 + [tʃ] [dʒ]
　　例：good job   old children's song   big challenge

Example 3. その他   [t] + [w] [r]、[v]+ [ð] など
　　例：that was   it rained   some of the students

Task 6   Listen to the following phrases and sentences, and read them aloud in pairs.   34

1. ancient record

2. tourist destination
3. That wasn't a good decision.
4. I decided to go ahead and buy a used bike.
5. It rained all night long yesterday.
6. What's the best way to get to Central Station?

Key Expressions

🎧 35

■ Expressions for Transition

- **In other words**, one in every five persons is infected with the virus.
  言い換えると、5人に1人がウイルスに感染していることになります。

- **As far as I know**, there aren't many children's books on environmental attitudes.
  私の知る限りでは、環境意識をテーマにした児童書はそんなに多くありません。

- **In contrast to** Japanese, English has the tradition of expressing everything frankly.
  日本語とは対照的に、英語は何でも率直に表現する伝統があります。

- **To illustrate** the point, I'll explain the procedure with the slide.
  ポイントを説明するために、スライドを使って手順を説明します。

- Japan is further along the road **when it comes to** disposing of plastic waste by category.
  プラスチックごみの分別処理の問題になると、日本のほうが進んでいます。

- **Apart from** that problem, what else can you suggest?
  その問題は別として、他に何か提案はありますか。

- The price of vegetables and fruit surged **owing to** extreme weather events around the world.
  世界中の極端な気象現象によって、野菜と果物の価格が急騰しました。

- **To sum up**, it's difficult to predict the future of nuclear energy.
  まとめると、原子力エネルギーの将来を予測することは困難だということです。

- **As a result**, the members of our project team left one by one.
  結果的に、プロジェクトメンバーは1人また1人とチームを去っていきました。

- **As a consequence of** global warming, average temperatures are rising in many parts of the world. 地球温暖化の結果、世界各地で平均気温が上昇しています。

Give It a Try! Mini-Presentation

1) First, listen to the Model below.
2) In pairs, read the Model paying attention to pronunciation and stress, rhythm, intonation, and sound changes in the passage.
3) After practicing, give peer feedback each other using the table below.

Model Ratio of Plastic to Fish in the Ocean   36

Do you know how much plastic is disposed of in the ocean? Although many of you don't know the exact amount, it is a problem we can't ignore. In other words, I hope you'll pay attention to one of the biggest environmental issues in the world after this presentation.

First, some people say that the world's oceans are polluted by plastic products. Plastic is useful and strong, and we use plastic products in our daily life. However, plastic such as PET bottles is often used only once and thrown away. As a result, the number of plastic products thrown away has been growing.

Second, according to the World Wide Fund for Nature Japan (WWF Japan) in 2018, about eight million tons of plastic are disposed of in the world's oceans year by year. To illustrate the situation, please look at the figure below. As you can see, the amount of plastic in the ocean is less than that of fish in 2014. However, by 2050, you'll find more plastic including invisible micro-plastic than fish. It is unfortunate that the natural environment has been damaged as a consequence of technological development.

It's important to encourage people not to throw garbage into the ocean in order to stop further ocean pollution. We need to cooperate to recover the natural environment of the ocean.

To sum up, the key to success in restoring the ocean depends on humans using fewer plastic products. Thank you for listening.

RATIO OF PLASTIC
TO FISH IN THE OCEAN

2014

2050

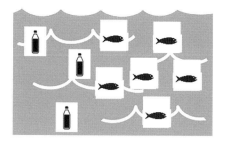
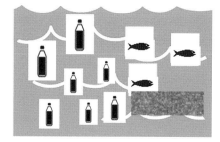

Rate the presentation on a scale from 1 to 4.

1: Fair   2: Good   3: Great   4: Excellent

Peer Feedback	Presenter's Name:		
	Circle the number for each item		Comments
Pronunciation (発音)	1 2 3 4		
Rhythm (Stress) (リズム・強勢)	1 2 3 4		
Intonation (抑揚)	1 2 3 4		

Peer Feedback	Presenter's Name:		
	Circle the number for each item		Comments
Pronunciation (発音)	1 2 3 4		
Rhythm (Stress) (リズム・強勢)	1 2 3 4		
Intonation (抑揚)	1 2 3 4		

Check (☑) what you have learned:

☐	how to pronounce a word with an appropriate stress
☐	the features of sound changes in phrases and sentences
☐	how to read aloud a presentation draft effectively

Unit 8　Telling Delivery

You will learn:

1. how to improve your presentation: volume, rhythm, and fluency
2. how to create an audio file of the script for shadowing
3. how to present 'Introduction/Conclusion' and provide feedback

Warm-up

 37

Tongue twisters are a great exercise to improve your pronunciation and fluency. Listen and try the following. Practice them and compete in pairs to see who can do it better!

1. Four fine fresh fish for you.
2. He threw three free throws.
3. I wish to wash my Irish wristwatch.
4. I saw a kitten eating chicken in the kitchen.
5. How much wood would a woodchuck chuck if a woodchuck could chuck wood?
6. If two witches would watch two watches, which witch would watch which watch?

どんなに立派な内容の発表でも、それが正しく伝わらなければ意味がありません。ここでは Unit 7 で学んだ英語らしい発音を活かし、しっかりした声量でより実践的な練習を行いましょう。

Key Point 1　Volume

すべての音に母音が伴われる日本語と違い、英語は十分な声量で話さなければ、子音が聞き取りにくくなります。英語を話すときは、いつも以上の声量でお腹から声を出す気持ちで発話するようにしましょう。

Task 1   Listen and fill in the blanks. 38

1) Listen to the audio and fill in the blanks below, remembering the "linking and consonant clusters" learned in the previous unit.

Let's say you are (¹   ) people you are not very close to.
(²   ) fact, you just (³   ) today! Do you have any
(⁴   ) for something fun to do?

2) Listen again and repeat at a sufficient volume.

母語の影響で、日本人は英語の子音に母音をつけて発音してしまいがちです。また、日本語にない子音を、似た他の音で代用してしまっていることもあります。自分の発音が正しく認識されるどうか、音声認識サービスやアプリ（e.g. AI 音声認識サービス **Notta**：右下の QR コード）をダウンロードして確認をしてみましょう。

Download the application to your smartphone. Press the X button and record your reading of the text above. Check if it is correctly spelled out.

If not, try again and again until you get it right!!

 Notta

Key Point 2   Rhythm

英語はとてもリズミカルな言語なので、英語特有のリズムを維持できる学習者ほど、その人の話す英語は、より自然かつ流暢に聞こえやすいと言われています。英語の自然なリズム習得のためには、言いよどむことのない流暢さ（fluency）や滑舌のよい鮮明さ（clarity）を確保することも大事です。このリズムが習得できると、英語のリスニング力さえ大幅にアップします。

では自分の発話をスマホのボイスメモで録音し、まずは自分の発話と客観的に向き合いましょう。スムーズに発話できるまで練習し、つぎにペアで話し合いましょう。

Task 2   Make an audio file of your speech.   39

I took a trip to Scotland and England when I was fifteen. I enjoyed visiting old churches and castles. However, my best memory there was watching a professional soccer game. The game was full of speed and excitement in the stadium.

1) Launch the *'Voice Memo'* on your smartphone and record the text above in your voice.
2) Listen to the audio and improve your speech as much as you can. (volume, fluency, clarity, rhythm, etc.)
3) In pairs, as you play it back, give peer feedback each other for the natural rhythm in English.

Key Point 3　　Shadowing Practice

自然な英語のリズムを習得する最も効率の良い方法に、パラレルリーディング（parallel reading）やシャドウイング（shadowing）があります。パラレルリーディングとは、ネイティブによるスピーチをよく聞いたあと、スピーチを聞きながら同時にスクリプトを音読することです。またシャドウイングとは、スクリプトを見ないで音声から1、2秒遅れて追いかけるようにスピーチすることです。シャドウイング練習の際には、段階的にまずスクリプトを見ながら行い、慣れてきたらスクリプトなしでシャドウイングするようにすればスムーズにできるようになります。では、次の英文を使って(1)〜(4)の手順で練習しましょう。

Task 3　Using the following text, practice steps (1) through (4).　 40

> The Wind Theater group is coming to Japan in August. This group has a worldwide reputation. Their musicals are performed in three languages: Japanese, English, and German. Their new story is written especially for the young, so I highly recommend it to everyone here.

1) While listening to the audio, read the passage silently to grasp the general meaning.
2) Read the text aloud along with the audio.（parallel reading）
3) Try shadowing the text as you look at it.
4) Shadow the text without looking at the text.（shadowing）

Key Expressions　　🎧 41

▦ Expressions in the First Person
● **I will focus on** the third point.
　3つ目のポイントに注目してみます。
● **I'd like to discuss** teleworking in Japan.
　日本のテレワークについて話したいと思います。

▦ Expressions with the Second Person
● **As you can see here**, there are three types of facial-recognition systems.
　このように、顔認識システムには3つのタイプがあります。
● **What you see here indicates** the recycling process of newspapers.
　ここに示されているのは、新聞のリサイクル工程です。

■ Expressions in the Imperative

- **Let's move on to** the next point.　次に進みましょう。
- **Let's take a look at** the next diagram.　次の図を見てみましょう。
- **Let me show you** how to operate this system.
  このシステムの操作方法をお見せします。
- **Take** the Industrial Revolution **as an example**.
  産業革命を例にとります。

■ Others

- **According to a survey**, there were 63 traffic accidents involving drivers aged 80 or over last year.　調査によると、昨年80歳以上のドライバーによる交通事故は63件でした。
- My car is made in Japan. **On the other hand**, yours is made in Germany.
  私の車は日本製です。一方、あなたの車はドイツ製です。

If your slides are your presentation, who needs you?

スライドがプレゼンだったら、あなたは必要ないってことになってしまうよね？

Give It a Try!　Mini-Presentation　

Unit 1 の 'Social Media and Personal Relationships' の introduction と conclusion を使ってスピーチ練習を行いましょう。ネイティブスピーカーの音声をよく聞き、シャドウイングがうまくできるようになったら、ペアやグループでスピーチを行い、評価シートを使ってフィードバックし合いましょう。

Model　Social Media and Personal Relationships (Introduction)　 42

Thank you very much, Professor Jones. Hello, everyone! I'm Ken Yamamoto from Powerful University. Today, I'd like to talk about 'Social Media and Personal Relationships.' Since we are digital natives, our smartphone is almost a part of our body, isn't it? I can't imagine a day without checking social media. But at the same time, these services can also hurt people if not used carefully and appropriately. So, first I will explain the background of current social media and describe the advantages and disadvantages of social networking. After that, I will explore the harmful effects the wrongful use of social media can have on personal relationships. Finally, I will try to show you the ideal relationship between social media and us.

Task **4**

1) Listen for the correct pronunciation and intonation. Mark the places of stress and pause.

2) Practice reading aloud, then do the parallel reading with the audio.

3) Try shadowing the speech looking at the script. Keep practicing until you can shadow it.

4) In pairs/groups, give a Mini-Presentation of the 'Introduction' and peer-feedback each other using the table below.

Rate the presentation on a scale from 1 to 4.

1: Fair   2: Good   3: Great   4: Excellent

Peer Feedback	Presenter's Name:		
	Circle the number for each item		Comments
Volume (声の大きさ)	1 2 3 4		
Fluency (流暢さ)	1 2 3 4		
Clarity (鮮明さ)	1 2 3 4		

つぎに、以下の **Conclusion** を使って同じように練習してみましょう。

Model   Social Media and Personal Relationships (Conclusion)   43

> In conclusion, while social networking sites can be a lot of fun, excessive use or wrong use can have harmful effects on personal relationships. So, I think we need to be very careful when using social media. As long as we use it appropriately, social media can always be a great fun tool, so let us use it with moderation. Thank you very much for your kind attention.

Task **5**

1) Listen for the correct pronunciation and intonation. Mark the places of stress and pause.

2) Practice reading aloud, then do the parallel reading with the audio.

3) Try shadowing the speech looking at the script. Keep practicing until you can shadow it.

4) In pairs/groups, give a Mini-Presentation of the 'Conclusion' and peer feedback each other using the table below.

Rate the presentation on a scale from 1 to 4.

1: Fair   2: Good   3: Great   4: Excellent

Peer Feedback	Presenter's Name:		
	Circle the number for each item		Comments
Volume （声の大きさ）	1 2 3 4		
Fluency （流暢さ）	1 2 3 4		
Clarity （鮮明さ）	1 2 3 4		

❗ Presentation Tips

ゆっくりと落ち着いた声で、語りかけるように話しましょう。強調したいときには声に抑揚をつけるだけでなく、少しポーズを置いてから話すと効果的です。

Check (☑) what you have learned:

☐	how to give a presentation in the appropriate volume and rhythm
☐	how to create an audio file of the script for shadowing
☐	how to present 'Introduction/Conclusion' and provide feedback

Unit 9　Non-verbal Communication

You will learn:

1. how to use effective eye contact to attract the audience
2. how to use suitable body language
3. how to have good posture while giving a talk

Warm-up

1. In groups, try gesture games. Choose one of the following topics that is of interest to you and try to describe it using gesture only. Do not use any words!

☐ countries　　　☐ movies　　　☐ sports
☐ technology　　☐ social issues　☐ part-time jobs

2. In groups, stand up and explain the same topic chosen above using English and gestures. Make sure you do not speak Japanese.

Key Point 1　　Three Types of Body Language

Eye contact

eye contact とは目と目（視線と視線）を合わせることです。発表を行う際、オーディエンスの注意を自分に惹きつけ、信頼関係を構築するという役割があります。一人一人の目を見て、語りかけるように話せば、オーディエンスとプレゼンターとの絆が生じます。その結果、一方的な発表にはならないでしょう。ゆっくりと、オーディエンス全体を見渡すことが大切です。

Gestures

body language の 1 つである gestures とは、スピーチに合わせて身体（主に手）を動かし、生き生きとした発表には欠かせないものです。物事を強調したり、順序立てて説明したり、あるいは口頭だけで不十分な時などに主に用いられます。また、顔の表情も gestures に含まれるため、深呼吸をしてリラックスし、笑顔でプレゼンテーションに臨みましょう。

Posture

posture とは発表を行う際の適切な姿勢のことです。両足を軽く開き、背筋を伸ばして話すことが望ましいと考えられています。演壇に寄りかかったり、猫背になったりせずに、堂々と話すことが求められます。

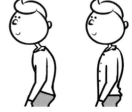

....

Task 1　Match the gestures exercises with the descriptions and illustrations below.

例：Make a fist with one hand and hit the palm of your other hand.

　　(d)(B)

1. Move one of your hands from an eye level position to a waist height position.

　　(　　)(　　)

2. Move your index finger diagonally upwards to above eye level.

　　(　　)(　　)

3. Hold your index, middle and ring fingers upwards in front of you.

　　(　　)(　　)

4. Hold your index finger pointing up with back of your hands facing outwards.

　　(　　)(　　)

5. Shrug your shoulders while holding your hands with the palms facing upwards on both sides of your body.

　　(　　)(　　)

a. Gesture indicating something low or short
b. Gesture indicating the number three
c. Gesture indicating a lack of understanding
d. Gesture emphasizing a point
e. Gestures indicating an increase
f. Gesture indicating a further point

Key Point 2   How to Use Body Language Effectively

Key Point 1 で学習した適切な body language を含んでいる動画を YouTube から検索して、比較します。

例1 「うつむいている」and「堂々と話している」

例2 身振り手振りが大袈裟なもの or トークに合わせて適切に身振り手振りを行っているもの

例3 姿勢が悪い発表 and 姿勢が良い発表

....

Task 2   Show pictures you have taken on iPad or smartphone in groups, then describe the photos using body language.

Key Point 3   Put into Practice! Let's Try to Make a Short Speech!

実際に与えられた speech に body language を付けて話してみましょう。

Task 3 Underline words and phrases where you think body language & gesture would be suitable to support your presentation. After reading the script on your own several times, perform it with your friends. In groups, make videos with your friends with body language. How could you take advantage of body language techniques? Focus on improving eye contact, gestures, and posture.

(sample)

    Thank you for your contributions to this intensive teambuilding program. To begin with, we have been making efforts throughout this program. Also, you are always being helpful and considerate. Above all, with Dr. Smith's initiatives, we have been able to learn essential communication and teamwork skills for success. Even for a short period of time, working closely together brought us fruitful opportunities to share unique and different perspectives. Hopefully, all of us will become successful in the future. Again, thank you very much for paying attention to my speech.

Key Expressions

 45

■ Expressions for Giving an Opinion

- **There are three main points** I would like to highlight. 　強調したいのは主に3つの点です。

- **First,** when I am in the library, I read **as many books as possible**.
  まず、図書館にいるとき、できるだけたくさんの本を読みます。

- **Next**, **watching movies is also an effective way to improve English**.
  次に、映画を観ることもまた、英語を上達させる効果的な方法です。

- **Third,** checking English-English dictionaries is **helpful for your learning**.
  3番目に、英英辞典で調べることはあなたの学習にとって、役に立ちます。

- During a recession, some have a hard time finding jobs, **no matter how hard** they try.
  景気後退の期間は、どれほど一生懸命になっても、仕事を見つけるのは難しいです。

- Some people think that studying mathematics and chemistry **would be no use**.
  数学や化学を学んでも役に立たないと考える人々もいます。

- **However, that is your own decision**. 　しかしながら、それはあなた自身が決めることです。

- **Move on to the next step**. 　次の段階へと進んでください。

- **Don't give up on your dream**. 　夢をあきらめないでください。

- **You should always tell yourself; "Yes, I can!"** いつも、「自分はできる」と信じるべきです。

Give It a Try! Mini-Presentation

Based on the Model, give a presentation using the Presentation Template below.

Let's try to make a presentation with body language!

1) Underline the words and phrases where you think body language & gesture would be suitable to support your presentation.

2) Then, read aloud and practice with body language on your own.

3) When you are ready, start peer assessment in groups.

Model How to Study English 46

Good morning, everyone. Today, I would like to talk about how I study English. There are **three main points** I would like to highlight.

First, when I have some free time, I watch YouTube **as much as possible**. There are many kinds of videos you can watch in English: news, documentaries, and TED Talks. Many of these have subtitles and I believe they are a really useful way to improve your vocabulary. And nowadays, because of smartphones, it's a really quick and convenient way to study.

Next, watching movies is also an effective way to improve your English. Of course, listening to natural speech in a movie can be a little difficult at first, but with practice you can really improve your listening skills. Another positive point is that it is a good way to learn about other cultures.

Finally, I would like to mention books. **Reading in English is really helpful**. Of course, reading will help you with your vocabulary but what you may not know is that **reading also helps you improve your writing skills**.

Many people believe that Japanese students cannot reach a high level of proficiency in English – **no matter how hard they try**. Indeed, some have even suggested that **the English education in Japan is a complete waste of time**.

However, I suggest that it's up to you. **Make your own decision**. Learning English is not easy. It takes time, and a lot of hard work. **Be realistic and set small goals for yourself**. Take it step by step. **With patience, you will find that this is a mountain you *can* climb**. Thank you for listening.

Presentation Template

Good morning, everyone. Today, I would like to talk about _____.

There are three main points I would like to highlight.

First, _____ as much as possible.

Next, _____ is an effective way to _____

_____.

Finally, I would like to mention _____. _____

also helps you improve your _____.

Many people believe that _____ cannot _____ – no

matter how _____ they try.

_____, it's up to you. It takes _____ and lots of

_____. Set _____ for yourself.

Don't give up on your dreams. Thank you for listening.

82

Rate the presentation on a scale from 1 to 4.

1: Fair   2: Good   3: Great   4: Excellent

Peer Feedback	Presenter's Name:				
	Circle the number for each item				Comments
Eye contact (アイコンタクト)	1	2	3	4	
Gestures (ジェスチャー)	1	2	3	4	
Posture (姿勢)	1	2	3	4	

Peer Feedback	Presenter's Name:				
	Circle the number for each item				Comments
Eye contact (アイコンタクト)	1	2	3	4	
Gesture (ジェスチャー)	1	2	3	4	
Posture (姿勢)	1	2	3	4	

Check (☑) what you have learned:

☐	how to use effective eye contact to attract the audience
☐	how to use suitable body language
☐	how to have good posture while giving a talk

Mission ③

Deliver Your Presentation!

Unit 7~9 で学習したことに基づき、最終プレゼンテーションに向けて仕上げの段階に入ります。あなた自身のプレゼンテーション原稿の音声ファイルを作成して練習することで、実際のスピーチを完成させていきましょう。

Step 1　Create your 'own' audio file and practice shadowing.

まず Mission 1 で作成した自分の発表スクリプトを音読練習しましょう。知らなかった単語を使用した場合、その発音を十分に確認してください。

1) Practice reading aloud, paying attention to the pronunciation of new words.

流暢に音読できるようになったら、発表原稿の音声ファイルを作りましょう。**英文読み上げソフト**（**e.g.** *Natural Reader*：**右下の QR コード**）をダウンロードし、発表原稿を入力します。話者の性別や英・米などの出身地、好きな声、声の調子さえ選ぶことができます。

2) Create the audio file of your 'own' presentation script using the application below. Listen for the correct pronunciation and intonation. Mark the places of stress & pause on your script.

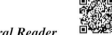

Natural Reader

音声ファイルは発話スピードも調整できます。自分のペースでパラレル・リーディングやシャドウイングを行いながら、自然な英語のリズムやイントネーションを習得しましょう。

3) Shadow along with it and keep practicing until you improve.

Step 2　Give your presentation using slides and body language.

それではグループに分かれ、Mission 2 で作成したスライドを提示しながら立ち上がって発表を行いましょう。

1) In pairs, practice your presentation, showing the slides and using gestures.

2) In groups, give your presentation and peer feedback each other using the tables below.

Presenter's Name: _____

Peer Feedback					
Effectiveness of slides スライドの明瞭さ	☹	🙁	😐	🙂	😊
Volume 声の大きさ	☹	🙁	😐	🙂	😊
Fluency 流暢さ	☹	🙁	😐	🙂	😊
Pronunciation 発音	☹	🙁	😐	🙂	😊
Posture 姿勢	☹	🙁	😐	🙂	😊
Eye contact アイコンタクト	☹	🙁	😐	🙂	😊
Gestures ジェスチャー	☹	🙁	😐	🙂	😊

Reviewer's Comments: _____

_____

_____

_____

_____

Presenter's Name: _____

Peer Feedback					
Effectiveness of slides スライドの明瞭さ	☹	☹	😐	🙂	😊
Volume 声の大きさ	☹	☹	😐	🙂	😊
Fluency 流暢さ	☹	☹	😐	🙂	😊
Pronunciation 発音	☹	☹	😐	🙂	😊
Posture 姿勢	☹	☹	😐	🙂	😊
Eye contact アイコンタクト	☹	☹	😐	🙂	😊
Gestures ジェスチャー	☹	☹	😐	🙂	😊

Reviewer's Comments: _____

_____

_____

_____

_____

Presenter's Name: _____

Peer Feedback					
Effectiveness of slides スライドの明瞭さ	☹	☹	😐	🙂	😊
Volume 声の大きさ	☹	☹	😐	🙂	😊
Fluency 流暢さ	☹	☹	😐	🙂	😊
Pronunciation 発音	☹	☹	😐	🙂	😊
Posture 姿勢	☹	☹	😐	🙂	😊
Eye contact アイコンタクト	☹	☹	😐	🙂	😊
Gestures ジェスチャー	☹	☹	😐	🙂	😊

Reviewer's Comments: _____

_____

_____

_____

_____

Unit 10 Q&A Session Strategies

You will learn:

1. how to ask and answer questions
2. the role of a moderator
3. how to interact with your audience effectively
4. how to use time effectively

Warm-up

You are the presenter. Your presentation is now finished. The moderator has started to take questions for a Q&A session. You have only five minutes for the Q&A session. A participant in the audience has started a long, digressive speech instead of asking a question. What would you do? Check (✓) the thing(s) you would do.

I would

☐ wait for him/her to finish his/her speech.

☐ tell him/her "I am sorry, but that is outside the area of this study".

☐ ask him/her "What is your question?"

Key Point 1   How to Ask and Answer Questions

....

Task 1   The following is an example from a Q&A session. Listen to the audio and fill in the gaps to match the Japanese.

M: Moderator   A: Audience   P: Presenter   🎧 47

M: Now, let's ＿＿＿＿＿ ＿＿＿＿＿ ＿＿＿＿＿ the question and answer session. ＿＿＿＿＿ ＿＿＿＿＿ have any questions or comments?

それでは、質疑応答に入らせていただきます。何かご質問あるいはご意見のある方はいらっしゃいませんか。

A: ＿＿＿＿＿ ＿＿＿＿＿ very much for your wonderful presentation. It was very interesting. I ＿＿＿＿＿ a question. You said fashion shows ...

88

素晴らしいご発表ありがとうございます。とても興味深かったです。1つ質問があります。ファッションは…

P: I'm sorry, but I _____ _____ you very well. _____ you please _____ that again?

すみませんが、あまりよく聞こえません。もう一度言っていただけますか。

A: Oh, I'm sorry. _____ _____ _____ environmental concerns are expressed through fashion today?

ああ、すみません。今も環境問題に関する懸念はファッションを通して表現されていると思いますか。

P: Yes. _____ _____ , we can see lots of advertisements every day. These days we often see 'sustainable' materials used for clothes.

はい。例えば、私たちは毎日広告を見ますが、最近は、服には「持続可能」な素材が使用されていることをよく見ますね。

A: _____ _____ . Thank you.

なるほど、わかりました。ありがとうございました。

M: Thank you. _____ _____ _____ or _____ , _____ ? Now let me _____ the session. Thank you for _____ _____ today.

ありがとうございました。他にご質問やご意見はありませんか。それでは、これで終了させていただきます。今日はご参加ありがとうございました。

Key Point 2   The Role of a Moderator

司会者は全体を見る必要があります。時間管理は大切で、プレゼンターの発表が終われば、質疑応答を受け付け、次のプレゼンターの時間が確保できるようにプレゼンターの持ち時間を管理しなければいけません。フロアから全く質問がでないときは積極的に質問することも司会者の重要な役割です。場の雰囲気を盛り上げたり、まとめたりできると素晴らしいです。

....

Task 2   The following expressions are often used by moderators and   🎧 48
presenters. Listen to the audio and fill in the gaps.

1. Now we'll _____ a question and answer session for _____ minutes.
2. _____ _____ _____ any questions?
3. Does anyone have any _____ on that?
4. _____ we _____ her a microphone?
5. I can _____ a couple more questions.
6. I'm afraid we are _____ _____ _____ _____ .

! Tips for moderators

1. 司会者は質疑応答の進行だけでなく、まず、オーディエンスに挨拶して、プレゼンターの紹介（名前、トピック）をします。プレゼンターが複数のときは、The next presenter (speaker) is... と言って、次のプレゼンターの紹介（名前、トピック）をします。

2. 司会者が time keeper の役割を担うことがあります。プレゼンテーションが 20 分以上の長い場合、終了予定の 5 分前に音で合図をするか、あと 5 分という紙をプレゼンターに見せて合図します。予め、プレゼンターと打ち合わせしておくといいでしょう。

3. フロアから質問が多くでることもあります。その場合は、時間がないので、次の質問で最後にしたいと伝え、最後の質問を受け付けるのもスムーズです。

Key Point 3 　　How to Interact with Your Audience Effectively

発表の後は、質疑応答があります。たまに質疑応答の時間を持てないほど、発表をしてしまう人がいますが、質疑応答の時間はオーディエンスの皆さんとの大切な出会いの場です。質疑応答を通して、オーディエンスの皆さんの関心や、質問に答えることができます。ひとりの質問を通して、オーディエンスの多くが発表の内容をより深く理解することもよくあります。

Task 3　　In pairs, practice a Q&A session. Tasks are written in the box.

Student A: **You are a moderator.**

Student B: **You are a presenter.**

Moderator's Tasks and Notes	Presenter's Tasks and Notes
Task 3.1 Introduce yourself as today's moderator. Tell the presenter that he or she will have 20 minutes for his/her presentation, followed by 5 minutes for a Q&A session.	Task 3.1 Greet the moderator and confirm how long today's presentation and Q&A session are. (_____ minutes for presentation, _____ minutes for a Q&A session)
Task 3.2 There is only one minute left for the presentation. Tell the presenter that he/she has only one minute left. How did the presenter react to the audience? The presenter said that _____ _____.	Task 3.2 In the middle of the presentation, the moderator said something to you. You did not hear it well, so ask what he/she has said. (What did the moderator say?) _____ _____

Task 3.3

The presenter has finished his/her presentation. Make a few comments and tell the audience that they have five minutes for the Q&A session, and then take questions.

Task 3.4

The presenter has finished the whole session. What did he/she say when closing it?

The presenter said that _____ .

Task 3.3

Your presentation is now finished. Thank the audience for listening to your presentation. Make eye contact with the moderator and wait for his/her instructions.

Task 3.4

Your presentation was very long and the time for the Q&A session is now over. However, several participants still want to ask questions. Apologize to the audience (including the moderator) and tell them that you are running out of time and if they have any questions, they can e-mail you later and you will answer them.

! Tips for a Q&A session

1. 決められた質疑応答の時間を確保できるように発表を準備しましょう。
2. 質問者の質問がとても長く、的を射た質問でないような場合は、「質問は何ですか」と聞き返すのも効果的です。
3. 時間がないときは、メールでの回答でもいいかと尋ねてみるのもいいです。
4. 短い質疑応答の時間を有効に使うには、スライドを画面に残しておき、すぐに質問の箇所が提示できるようにしておくとスムーズです。

Key Point 4   How to Use Time Effectively

時間には限りがあります。無限に時間があれば、延々とコミュニケーションできますが、現実はそうではないので、発表の持ち時間をうまく使うことが大切になってきます。

Task 4

93 ページの Give It a Try! 〈Mini-Presentation〉 のリハーサルをしましょう。

Student A: **You are a presenter.**

Rehearse with your classmate and fill out the box below.

Student B: **You are a listener.**

Listen to your classmate rehearse, ask questions if necessary and give some feedback. Then, fill out the box below.

Presenter's Notes	Listener's Notes
Listener's name:	Presenter's name:
● Listener's feedback:	● What's the topic?
● Your own feedback: (e.g., How would you like to give a presentation differently next time?)	● Your comments:

⚠ Tips for presenters

1. Rehearse and prepare for a better performance. 発表のリハーサルをして、気づきを得ましょう。誰もリハーサルに付き合ってくれない時は、スマホで録音して、質疑応答の時間をきちんと残せるかかっておくのもおすすめです。

2. Predict the questions you are likely to be asked and prepare answers. リハーサルが終わると聞かれそうな質問を予想できるようになります。聞かれないかも知れませんが、準備しておくことで、質疑応答の際はスムーズに答えられるでしょう。

Key Expressions

🎧 49

▌▌▌Expressions for Managing Q&A Sessions

- **We'll have a question and answer session at the end of the presentation.**
  プレゼンテーションの終わりに質疑応答のセッションがあります。

- Now **we'll have a question and answer session for** five **minutes**.
  今から質疑応答のセッションを5分間持ちたいと思います。

- **Does anyone have any questions?** ご質問はありますか。

- **Any other questions?** 他にご質問はありますか。

- **Does that answer your questions?** 答えになっていますでしょうか。

- **I can take a couple more questions.** あと2、3質問を受けられます。

- **I'm afraid we are running out of time.** 残念ながら時間がなくなってしまいました。

- **If you have more questions, I would be happy to** answer them by e-mail.
  まだご質問があれば、喜んでメールでお答えします。

■ Expressions for Asking Questions

● **Thank you for your** wonderful **presentation. I have** a **question.**
素晴らしいご発表ありがとうございました。1つ質問があります。

● **May (Can) I ask you a question?** 質問してもいいですか。

● **Could you be more specific about your** second **point**?
2つ目の点についてもっと具体的に教えてくれますか。

Give It a Try! Mini-Presentation

Based on the Model, give a presentation, using the Presentation Template below. Let's talk about our favorite books.

Model My Favorite Book 50

> Today, I would like to introduce my favorite book called *Never Let Me Go* by Kazuo Ishiguro. I read it last month. It was very interesting. The main character is a young woman called Kathy. She grew up in a boarding school. Children in the boarding school are all clones. Kathy and her friends grow up and they find out their destiny. They are destined to be organ donors and will die or "complete". I enjoyed the book. It was a sad story, but it made me think about clones. **Thank you for** listening. **Now, we'll have a question and answer session for** two **minutes. Do you have any questions?**

Presentation Template

> Today, I would like to introduce my favorite book called _____ by _____.
> It's (a) _____ (e.g., mystery, romance, tragedy).
> The main character(s) is/are _____ (e.g., a young woman called Kathy. She grew up in a boarding school.).
> _____ _____ _____ (e.g., Children in the boarding school are all clones. Kathy and her friends grow up and they find out their destiny. They are destined to be organ donors and will die or "complete".)
> I like the book/I enjoyed the book because _____ (e.g., The ending was surprising. The book was realistic. It was a sad story, but it made me think about clones.). Thank you for listening. Now, we will have a question and answer session for _____ minutes. Do you have any questions?

Evaluation Form   Mini-Presentation で学んだことを振り返ってみよう！
Check (☑) the boxes.

	Yes	No
1. Did you rehearse and receive feedback as a presenter?	☐	☐
2. Did you predict the questions you were likely to be asked and prepare answers as a presenter?	☐	☐
3. Did you thank the audience as a presenter/moderator?	☐	☐
4. Did you conduct a Q&A session smoothly as a presenter/moderator?	☐	☐
5. Did you ask questions as a participant?	☐	☐

Check (☑) what you have learned:

☐	how to ask and answer questions
☐	the role of a moderator
☐	how to interact with your audience effectively
☐	how to use time effectively

Unit 11　Rehearsal and Practice

You will learn:

1. where to improve with video clips
2. checkpoints in rehearsals
3. what to practice for the final presentation

Key Point 1　　Video Examples of Presentation

プレゼンテーションのさまざまな実例を見て、よかった点、改善が必要な点を話し合いましょう。
そして、自分のプレゼンテーションを改善しながら、練習を重ねましょう。

Task 1

Watch the video clips and evaluate them.

 List of video clips

Video A	Your Comment
Before 1 	

Before 2 		**After** 

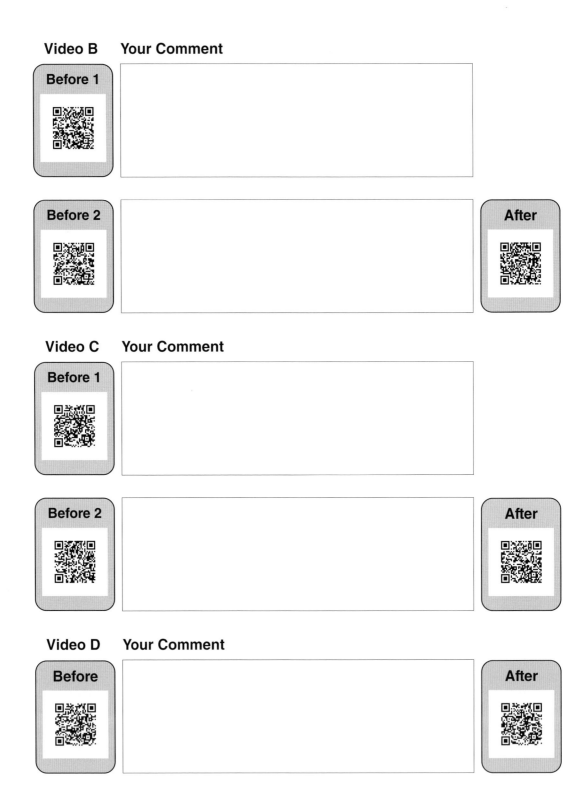

Video B   **Your Comment**

Before 1

Before 2

After

Video C   **Your Comment**

Before 1

Before 2

After

Video D   **Your Comment**

Before

After

Video E　　**Your Comment**

Video F　　**Your Comment**

Key Point 2　　Rehearsal

練習を重ねたら、本番の環境に近い状態でリハーサルを行います。リハーサルの段階で必要な次のような準備も合わせて確認しておきましょう。

配布資料の準備

プレゼンテーションの資料を配布する場合は、必要部数を確認したうえで印刷し、ホッチキスで留めるところまでを事前に完了しておきます。

会場確認

初めて使用する会場の場合は、本番前に下見をしましょう。部屋の広さ、会場のレイアウトを見て、オーディエンス全員がスクリーンがよく見えることをチェックし、また会場にどんな設備があるか（PC、プロジェクター、マイクの設置やインターネットの接続環境など）を確認します。

機器の確認

下見の際は、自分が使う機器で動作確認をしましょう。実際に使用するPCとプロジェクターを接続して、一番後の席からスライドが見えるどうか、音声が聞こえるかどうかをチェックします。特に文字のサイズと色、スライドの見やすさの確認は大切です。

¥持ち物

当日の持ち物も早めに準備しておきましょう。USBメモリ、時計、Q&A用のメモとペンなど、必要に応じて用意しておきます。

¥Q&A session 対策

質問にうまく対応できないと、発表全体の失敗という印象が残ることもあります。そこで、答えられない場合の対策も考えておきましょう。リハーサルのときに出た質問を想定質問としてその回答を準備し、再リハーサルでその質問に答えるという練習をしておくとよいでしょう。

Task 2

1. Perform the presentation, showing the slides and using gestures.
2. Watch the presentations of your group and fill out the Checklist below.
3. Give each other advice on each presentation.

Peer-Assessment Checklist

Presenter' Name　＿＿＿＿＿＿＿＿＿＿＿＿＿＿＿＿＿

Title　＿＿＿＿＿＿＿＿＿＿＿＿＿＿＿＿＿＿＿＿＿＿＿＿

●Contents
- ☐ トピックの導入はわかりやすかったか。
- ☐ 各ポイントの説明はわかりやすかったか。
- ☐ 結論はわかりやすかったか。

●Visuals
- ☐ スライドは見やすいものだったか。
- ☐ 図解やチャートを活用していたか。

●Delivery
- ☐ 発音は適切だったか。
- ☐ 流暢に話せていたか。
- ☐ 声の大きさは適切だったか。
- ☐ ジェスチャー・アイコンタクト
- ☐ 姿勢は適切だったか。

●Interaction with Audience
- ☐ 原稿の内容を暗記して発表できたか。
- ☐ 時間内に終えることができたか。

Key Point 3   Practice! Practice! Practice!

プレゼンテーションの成否の度合いは、どれだけ入念に準備をしたかに正比例します。これから次のような準備を行って本番に臨みましょう。

1. Examples, TED talks

さまざまなプレゼンテーションの実例を見て、参考にしましょう。特にお勧めしたいのが TED Talks です。さまざまな分野の第一線で活躍する人の優れたプレゼンテーションを、インターネットで無料視聴することができます。

TED talks を 5 本以上視聴して、自分のプレゼンテーションの参考になると思ったことをメモしましょう。

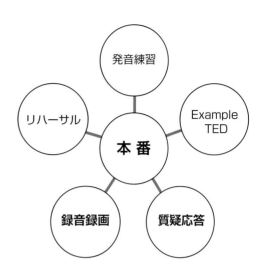

Presenter & Title	参考にしたいところ

2. 発音練習

基本的にはすべての原稿を覚えて、自然に話すことができるようになるまで練習しましょう。その際、個々の単語の発音だけでなく、イントネーションやストレスにも注意します。そして、音声認識アプリ（巻末 Appendix 収録の QR コード①）を使って録音し、発表時間を計ってみましょう。

3. リハーサル

本番を想定したリハーサルはあらゆる機会をとらえて繰り返し行います。p. 98 の Checklist を活用しながら、お互いに評価し合いましょう。

4. 質疑応答

プレゼンテーション後の質問に対して英語で的確に応答するのは容易ではありません。
事前に想定できる質問とその回答をできるだけたくさん考えておきましょう。

5. 録音・録画

練習はスマートフォンで録音または録画します。自分で振り返ってみると、発音が不明確だとか、ジェスチャーが不自然だなどと、改善すべき点が必ず見つかります。

Check (☑) what you have learned:

☐	where to improve with video clips
☐	checkpoints in rehearsals
☐	what to practice for the final presentation

Unit 12   Final Presentation

You will learn:

1. what points to check before the presentation
2. how to evaluate your classmate's presentation
3. how to reflect on your own presentation

Warm-up

Anyone can feel anxious when giving a presentation but each person may have some tips to reduce presentation anxiety. Share them in groups.

Name	Tips
(e.g.) NOMURA Tadakazu	Drink water to calm down.

Close your eyes for one minute to visualize your success in delivering the presentation. After visualization, share your image and how you feel in your group.

Your image	How you feel
(e.g.) During the presentation, I often have eye-contact with the audience!	(e.g.) Because they are listening, I feel excited to speak to them.

Key Point 1　Final Presentation Checklist

発表本番では、予期せぬ問題に直面することがあります。Unit 11 で発表の練習を行いましたが、ここでは発表本番に起こり得る問題に備え、これから行うプレゼンテーションの前に確認しておくこととプレゼンテーション中に気をつけることを述べます。

Task 1　Read each statement below. When you have confirmed them, check (☑) the box.

Before the presentation	
☐	教室の明るさは（カーテン・照明等で調整できる場合は調整して）適切だ。
☐	発表時に立つ場所（スクリーンの横か演台の後ろか）を確認した。
☐	配布資料の置き場所を確認し、資料は十分にある。
☐	配布資料は順番通りに綴じられている。
☐	自分のパソコンを使う場合、バッテリー残量や電源の位置を確認した。
☐	自分のパソコンを使う場合、スライドがスクリーン上で適切に表示されている。
☐	スライドで使用するアニメーション・動画・音声はうまく機能している。
☐	マイクやレーザーポインターは問題なく作動している。
☐	インターネットを使用する場合、接続はできている。
☐	Q&A 用のメモとペンがある。
☐	発表時間計測の時計がある。
During the presentation	
☐	発表の際には、オーディエンス全体を見る（時折、熱心な人の目を見て話す）。
☐	笑顔・姿勢・ジェスチャーを意識的に確認する。
☐	声の大きさ・話すスピード・声のトーン・間合いに気をつける。
☐	熱意・自信を持って話す。
☐	ミスをしたら、深呼吸をして再開する。
☐	教室の最後尾の人に（必要ならばマイクを用いて）声が届く。

❗ Presentation Tips

適度な緊張や不安は必要

プレゼンテーションをする際に緊張や不安を感じない人はいないでしょう。緊張しすぎると、言おうとしたことを忘れることはよくあります。「ヤーキーズ・ドッドソンの法則」によれば、高すぎず低すぎない適度な緊張が成功につながると言われます。不安があるからこそ、前もって準備をしたり練習をしたり、丁寧にわかりやすい発表を心がけたり、真剣な面持ちで発表をしたりするので、かえって発表がうまくいき、真剣度や熱意が伝わることがあります。自分にとっての「適度な」緊張・不安を理解するようにしましょう。

❶ Presentation Tips

Filler（フィラー）を効果的に！

Filler（フィラー）とは、「えーっと」「あー」「うーん」といった話の最中につい口から出てくる本題とは関係のない言葉のことです。発表中に何を言うか考えようと沈黙するよりも、これらの表現をうまく使うことで話の流れがスムーズになります。英語でプレゼンテーションをする際にも、日本語で言うのではなく、英語で「uh（アー）」「um（アーム）」「well（ウェル）」「Let me see」などの表現を使うようにしてみましょう。一方で、話のポイントがわからなくなることもありますので、使いすぎには気をつけましょう。

Key Point 2　Peer Evaluation

自分のプレゼンテーションがうまくいったかどうかについて客観的に振り返るのは難しいものです。そのため、聴いてくれた相手にあなたのプレゼンテーションの長所と短所を尋ねるのが一番です。また逆に、他の人のプレゼンテーションを観察し、長所と短所についてフィードバックを与えることは、自分が参考にすべき点や改善すべき点に気づくことになるので、あなた自身のプレゼンテーションの上達につながります。

フィードバックを与える際には以下の点に気をつけます。

● 長所・短所両方についての具体的なアドバイス：フィードバックが具体的でないと、プレゼンターの長所短所がわかりにくくなります。

● 短所の指摘は2～4割程度：短所ばかりを指摘されると自信を失ったり嫌な気持ちになったりするので、少なめにします。

● 建設的なアドバイス：短所については、改善点も併せて指摘することが重要です。

Task 2 Evaluate your classmate's presentation based on the points studied in this textbook. Circle the appropriate number of each phase and give comments about strengths and weaknesses of his/her presentation.

Evaluation Form

Date: 20 ____ / _____ / _____

Presenter's Name: _____

Title: _____

	Fair	Good	Great	Excellent
Contents				
・Introduction（導入）				
・Body（本文）	1	2	3	4
・Conclusion（結論）				
Visuals				
・Slides（スライド）	1	2	3	4
・Diagrams / Charts（図解・グラフ）				
Delivery				
・Pronunciation（発音）				
・Fluency（流暢さ）				
・Volume（声の大きさ）	1	2	3	4
・Non-verbal Communication （非言語コミュニケーション）				
Interaction with Audience				
・Q&A（質疑応答）	1	2	3	4
・Timekeeping（時間厳守）				

Total Score: (　　　　) / 16

Advice:

(e.g.) *You explained details of your topic well. However, as you spoke quickly, I couldn't catch some words. Please speak more slowly.*

Key Point **3**　Self-reflection

自分のプレゼンテーションが終わりオーディエンスからフィードバックをもらった後は、プレゼンテーションスキルの向上に向けて、自分のプレゼンテーションを振り返ることが大切です。振り返りの際には次の点に注意を払います。

● 長所は何か：どのようにすればさらによくなるかを考えます。
● 短所は何か：もらったフィードバックすべてを受け入れる必要はありませんが、多くの人から言われていることについては対応する必要があります。フィードバックで言われていないことでも、自己分析してうまくいかなかった点を考えます。

Task **3**　Reflect on your presentation and write down your strengths and weaknesses.

Strength:

(e.g.) My charts were easy to understand. To develop my skills on visual aid use, I would like to learn other types of charts.

Weakness:

(e.g.) I didn't use gestures often. It would be good to learn what gestures can be useful for the presentation.

Key Expressions

🎧 51

■ Expressions for the Reflection on Strengths

● Effectively delivering my opinions in understandable English **was one of my strong points.**
自分の意見をわかりやすい英語で効果的に伝えることは、私の長所の１つでした。

● **I was excellent at** presenting information in charts.
グラフでの情報提示が非常に得意でした。

● **The good point about my presentation was** that I could successfully organize a lot of information effectively into a few slides.　私のプレゼンテーションの良かった点は、多くの情報を効果的に数枚のスライドにうまくまとめられたことでした。

▥ Expressions for the Reflection on Weaknesses

● **I think I should have given** more details about the first reason.
1 つ目の理由については、もっと詳しく**説明すべきだった**と思います。

● **One of my weak points was** that I didn't speak clearly.
私の弱点の 1 つは、はっきりとした話し方ができていなかったことでした。

● **I'm afraid that I couldn't** handle questions from the audience after the presentation.
発表後、オーディエンスからの質問に対応できなかったのが残念です。

▥ Expressions for Encouragement

● **Excellent / Brilliant / Well done / Good job**!
素晴らしい / 見事です / よくできました / よく**頑張りました**！

● I think **you made a good presentation**.
いいプレゼンテーションだったと思います。

● **I was impressed with** how well organized your presentation was.
プレゼンテーションの構成がよくまとまっていることに**感心しました**。

● Your presentation has helped me think about the results. **Keep it up!**
あなたのプレゼンテーションは結果について考えるのに役立ちました。**その調子で頑張ってください**！

Give It a Try! Mini-Reflection

Based on the Model, share the reflection about your own presentation in pairs using the Reflection Template. Remember that after listening to the partner's reflection, respond to it by expressing praise/encouragement. When you have finished, switch roles.

Model Self-reflection on Your Presentation 52

Student A: **My presentation was about** my hometown. **The good point was** that my explanation was logical and had lots of examples. I believe this made my audience understand my argument well. **On the other hand, one of my weak points was** color use in my slides. Because I used yellow a lot, it seemed that the audience couldn't see words and numbers clearly. So I would like to improve this.

Student B: **Your presentation** gave me lots of food for thought. **Keep it up!**

Reflection Template

Student A: My presentation was about _____.
        The good point was _____.
        On the other hand, one of my weak points was _____.
Student B: Your presentation _____. Keep it up!

Check (☑) what you have learned:

☐	what points to check before the presentation
☐	how to evaluate my classmate's presentation
☐	how to reflect on my presentation

Optional Unit　Various Presentations

You will learn:

1. how to create a poster presentation
2. how to give a Zoom presentation
3. how to play a presentation on iPad

Warm-up

1. In groups, choose a topic you find interesting and draw pictures on some paper. Make a story, but do not use any language!

   ☐ countries　　　☐ movies　　　☐ sports
   ☐ technology　　☐ social issues　☐ part-time jobs

2. In groups, stand up and explain the pictures and the story in English. Make sure you do not speak Japanese.

Key Point 1　　New Types of Presentation

Poster presentation

Poster presentation, Poster session では、プレゼンターは視覚的効果を最大限に活用して、研究成果の一部や実践に焦点を当てて報告できます。文字のフォントを大きくして、コンテンツを端的に示したポスターがより効果的です。また、プレゼンターとオーディエンスの距離が近いため、気軽な質疑応答が可能で、オーディエンスはその場で発表内容の理解を深め、インタラクティブな情報交換ができます。準備段階では、オーディエンスに興味を持ってもらえるデザイン性に富んだ、ポスターを作成します。

Zoom presentation

オンライン化が中心となり、今や Zoom の活用は当然のことのようになりました。映像や音声を用いて、授業、会議、学会等の実施が可能です。Zoom を使用すれば、いつでも、どこでも、世界中の人々とオンライン上でつながり、自分の研究内容を共有することができます。Zoom presentation では、画面共有のため、Non-verbal language は必要ありません。効果的な PowerPoint slides が求められます。

iPad presentation

全員の学生が1人1台 iPad を用いて、presentation を行うことも対面授業においては珍しくなくなりました。iPad 上での PowerPoint の再生方法を学びましょう。そして、授業内で iPad を用いた presentation をしましょう。

Task 1 The descriptions for Poster presentation are given. Put them into the correct order. Then, match those descriptions with illustrations below.

1. The content is consistent, and use clear and simple language.　　　(　)

2. The text on the slide is clear. Don't include too much information.　　(　)

3. The title is short and large enough to be readable from far away.　　 (　)

4. Use effective visual aids such as graphics, colors, and charts.　　　 (　)

5. Answer questions from the audience, and communicate well.　　　　(　)

6. Make the poster read left to right just like a page.　　　　　　　 (　)

　　Order: (　) → (　) → (　) → (　) → (　) → (　)

A

B

C

D

E

F

Task 2 The descriptions for Zoom meetings are given. Put them into the correct order. Then, match those descriptions with the illustrations below.

1. Create a presentation in PowerPoint on a PC.   (   )

2. Send a passcode to participants for the Zoom meeting.   (   )

3. Start the slideshow.   (   )

4. Share your screen with participants during live sessions. (   )

5. Join a Zoom meeting.   (   )

6. Ask questions using chat.   (   )

   Order: (   ) → (   ) → (   ) → (   ) → (   ) → (   )

A

B

C

D

E

F

Key Point **2**   Make Presentations Using an iPad or a Smartphone!

プレゼンテーションを作成した後、iPad または smartphone を用いて教室でプロジェクターに提示します。

Task **3**   Make Slides such as PowerPoint, Google Slides, or Keynote on iPad or smartphone. Then, show the slides on screen and make a presentation with body language.

Key Expressions 53

■ Expressions for Opening Remarks

● **Can everyone hear me?**　皆さん、聞こえますか？

● **Let me share the slide.**　スライドを共有させてください。

● **A large number of people have changed their working styles** during the COVID pandemic.　コロナ禍において、**大多数の人々が働き方を変えました**。

■ Expressions for Charts

● **Look at the line chart. Gradually, people are switching to a remote work style.** 折れ線グラフをご覧ください。次第に、人々はリモートワークへと働き方を変えています。

● **The bar chart shows what kinds of goods** consumers tend to choose at the supermarket.　**棒グラフを見れば**、消費者がスーパーマーケットでどのような**商品を選ぶ傾向**にあるかということが**わかります**。

● **Obviously, with technological development**, modern society has become more convenient and efficient in all aspects.　明らかに、**技術の発展に伴って**、現代社会はあらゆる側面において、より便利で効率的になっています。

■ Expressions for Concluding Remarks

● **Under these circumstances**, people have to be aware of their own safety. このような状況では、人々は自分自身の安全性を意識しなければなりません。

● **Moreover, technological development might have positive effects on** our daily life. さらに、**科学技術の発展は**、私たちの日常生活に**肯定的な影響を与えています**。

● **In the future, their specific contributions to** the local government **will be more precisely analyzed.**　将来的に、地方自治体に対する具体的な貢献度を、より綿密に分析していくことでしょう。

● **If you have any questions, please share them in the chat box.** もしご質問があれば、チャットボックスで共有してください。

Give It a Try!   Mini-Presentation

Based on the Model, give a presentation using the Presentation Template below.

Let's try to make a Zoom presentation!

1) Choose a topic for your presentation.

2) Then, write a script and use a bar chart, a line chart, or a pie chart to summarize data based on your research topic.

3) Create a PowerPoint slide. When you are ready, work on your Zoom presentation.

Model   Business During COVID-19 54

> Good afternoon, thank you for coming to my Zoom presentation. **Can everyone hear me**? I am Hanako Tanaka, majoring in business. Today, I am talking about business during COVID-19. **Let me share the slide.** Due to the COVID-19 pandemic, **a large number of people have changed their working styles**. Whereas some were required to get different jobs, others started flexible work schedules at home. **Look at the line chart**. **Gradually, people are switching to a remote work style.**
>
> Also, since COVID-19, consumers tend to utilize online shopping. Some companies might benefit from the pandemic. Therefore, I have been researching ABC company's sales performance online. Since COVID-19, the sales have been dramatically rising. In addition, **the bar chart shows what kinds of goods** consumers have purchased online since 2019. **Obviously, with technological development**, PCs are necessary for customers' work and private use.
>
> A large number of remote workers have tended to stay home since COVID-19. **Under these circumstances**, consumers prefer shopping online to visiting stores. **Moreover, technological development might have positive effects on** the production of electronics.
>
> **So far, I have only discussed part of my research,** the online sales performance of ABC company. **In the future, their specific contributions to** the economic development in the local areas **will be more precisely analyzed**. Thank you for your attention. **If you have any questions, please share them in the chat box**.

Title slide (1)

Outline slide (2)

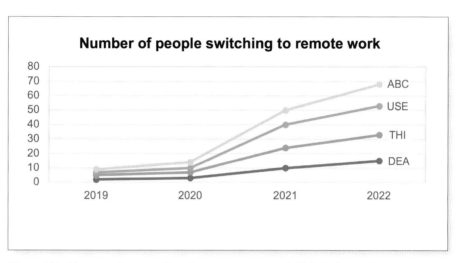

Note: 折れ線グラフ上の ABC, USE, THI, DEA は会社名を表します。

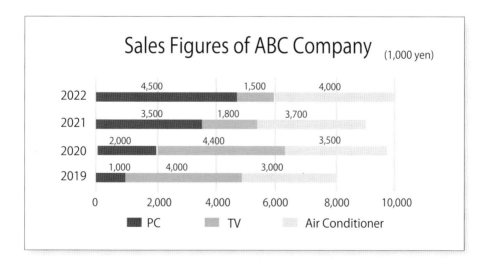

Conclusion slide

References slide

Presentation Template

Good afternoon, thank you for coming to my Zoom presentation. Today, I am talking about _____. Let me share the slide. Look at _____ . _____

_____ .

Also, _____ . In addition, _____ . _____

_____ .

Moreover, _____ . So far, I have only discussed part of my research, _____. Thank you for your attention. If you have any questions, please share them in the chat box.

! Presentation Tips

オンライン・プレゼンテーションは Zoom の他にも Google Meet, Microsoft Teams などが用いられます。その場で求められる Learning Management System（LMS）、すなわち学習管理システムを使いこなして、プレゼンテーションに取り組みましょう。

Rate the presentation on a scale from 1 to 4.

1: Fair　　2: Good　　3: Great　　4: Excellent

Peer Feedback	Presenter's Name:				
	Circle the number for each item				Comments
Slide （スライド）	1	2	3	4	
Voice Delivery （音声）	1	2	3	4	
Content （内容）	1	2	3	4	
Organization （構成）	1	2	3	4	
Language （言語）	1	2	3	4	

Peer Feedback	Presenter's Name:				
	Circle the number for each item				Comments
Slide （スライド）	1	2	3	4	
Voice Delivery （音声）	1	2	3	4	
Content （内容）	1	2	3	4	
Organization （構成）	1	2	3	4	
Language （言語）	1	2	3	4	

Check (☑) what you have learned:

☐	how to create a poster presentation
☐	how to give a Zoom presentation
☐	how to play a presentation on iPad

執筆者

JACET 関西支部教材開発研究会

松村　優子	(まつむら　ゆうこ)	Pre-Unit, Unit 2, 3, Mission 1 【第 17 次プロジェクト代表】
香林　綾子	(こうばやし　あやこ)	Unit 4, 10 【第 17 次プロジェクト副代表】
大内　和正	(おおうち　かずまさ)	Unit 5, 11, Mission 2
杉本　喜孝	(すぎもと　よしたか)	Pre-Unit, Unit 7
田口　達也	(たぐち　たつや)	Unit 6, 12
仲川　浩世	(なかがわ　ひろよ)	Unit 9, Optional Unit
幸重美津子	(ゆきしげ　みつこ)	Unit 1, 8, Mission 3

英文校閲者

Howard Jones （ハワード・ジョーンズ）

新・英語でプレゼンテーション

2024 年 2 月 20 日　　第 1 版発行

著　者 ——— JACET 関西支部教材開発研究会
発行者 ——— 前田俊秀
発行所 ——— 株式会社 三修社
　　　　　　〒 150-0001 東京都渋谷区神宮前 2-2-22
　　　　　　TEL 03-3405-4511　FAX 03-3405-4522
　　　　　　振替 00190-9-72758
　　　　　　https://www.sanshusha.co.jp
　　　　　　編集担当 三井るり子
印刷所 ——— 壮光舎印刷株式会社

©2024 Printed in Japan ISBN978-4-384-33532-3 C1082

表紙デザイン ———— 峯岸孝之
本文デザイン・DTP —— 有限会社トライアングル
準拠音声制作 ———— 高速録音株式会社

教科書準拠 CD 発売
本書の準拠 CD をご希望の方は弊社までお問い合わせください。